FAMILY PROVISION:
LAW AND PRACTICE

AUSTRALIA AND NEW ZEALAND
The Law Book Company Ltd.
Sydney : Melbourne : Perth

CANADA AND U.S.A.
The Carswell Company Ltd.
Agincourt, Ontario

INDIA
N.M. Tripathi Private Ltd.
Bombay
and
Eastern Law House Private Ltd.
Calcutta and Delhi
M.P.P. House
Bangalore

ISRAEL
Steimatzky's Agency Ltd.
Jerusalem : Tel-Aviv : Haifa

MALAYSIA : SINGAPORE : BRUNEI
Malayan Law Journal (Pte.) Ltd.
Singapore

PAKISTAN
Pakistan Law House
Karachi

FAMILY PROVISION: LAW AND PRACTICE

by

John G. Ross Martyn, B.A., LL.B. (CANTAB.)

of the Middle Temple and Lincoln's Inn,
Barrister

Second Edition

LONDON
Sweet & Maxwell
1985

First Edition   1978
Second Edition   1985

Published by
Sweet & Maxwell Limited of
11 New Fetter Lane, London.
Computerset by Burgess & Son (Abingdon) Limited.
Printed in Great Britain by
Eyre & Spottiswoode Ltd, Thanet Press, Margate

British Library Cataloguing in Publication Data

Ross Martyn, John G.
    Family provision: law and practice.—2nd ed.
    1. Decedents' family maintenance—England
    I. Title   II. Ross Martyn, John G. Modern law of
    family provision
    344.2064   KD1515 F3
    ISBN 0–421–34280–3

Preface

This book is a new and much enlarged edition of *The Modern Law of Family Provision*, published in 1978, and incorporated with amendments in the 1982 edition of *Williams, Mortimer and Sunnucks on Executors, Administrators and Probate*.

I hope that the Appendices will be useful. Dickensians must excuse the names used in the precedents in Appendix 4, as a Chancery Barrister's puny attempt at revenge for "Bleak House." Appendix 5 includes all the reported cases on the 1975 Act and its predecessors that I have been able to trace, but I would welcome information about any I have missed.

I would also welcome constructive criticism of the book. It was common, in more specious days, for authors of lawbooks to state that the responsibility for any shortcomings was their own. Nevertheless, I have to emphasise that, although I have used my best endeavours to be accurate, I can accept no legal responsibility for any mistakes in the book.

Now to my thanks. I am very grateful to Master Dyson for his help in perusing the proofs of this edition and making a number of helpful suggestions. More generally, my thoughts and ideas about the family provision jurisdiction owe a great deal to discussion with other members of the Bar, in my own Chambers especially, but also elsewhere. I thank them all. It would be invidious of me to select any for specific mention by name, except perhaps Peter Mottershead, Q.C. because his untimely death has prevented him from reading my general words of thanks.

In the preface to the first edition I thanked my wife for her tolerance of the time taken up by the writing of the book. I now have the pleasure of thanking both her and my children likewise, in relation to this new edition.

Lincoln's Inn   John Ross Martyn
October, 1985

Contents

Table of Cases

Table of Statutes

1 Introduction

General

The Inheritance (Provision for Family and Dependants) Act 1975 (referred to hereafter as "the 1975 Act" or "the Act" according to context) replaces both the Inheritance (Family Provision) Act 1938[1] as amended ("the 1938 Act"), and sections 26, 27 and 28 of the Matrimonial Causes Act 1965[1] ("the 1965 Act"). The 1975 Act changes the old law as embodied in the 1938 and 1965 Acts substantially, so as to form a new and comprehensive code of family provision law. However, it gives the court essentially the same power as that given by the 1938 and 1965 Acts,[2] that is a discretionary power to re-write a particular will or alter the effect of the statutory rules of intestacy in a particular case, so as to make reasonable provision for members of what might be called the "family circle" of the deceased. The new Act entitles certain persons,[3] who were linked to a deceased person by ties of marriage, blood or dependence, to apply to the court on the ground that the disposition of the deceased's estate effected by his will or the law relating to intestacy or a combination of the two is not such as to make reasonable financial provision for them. If the court agrees that reasonable financial provision has not been made for any such applicant, it may order what it considers reasonable financial provision to be made for that applicant out of the estate of the deceased.

Although the law recognises that the deceased may have been

---

[1] For the 1938 and 1965 Acts, see the 10th ed. of Williams, Mortimer and Sunnucks, *Executors, Administrators and Probate*, pp. 539–550; Theobald, *The Law of Wills*, 13th ed., 1971, paras. 321–356; Tyler, *Family Provision*. This last gives a very full treatment. It is referred to hereafter as Tyler. The second edition, which states the law as at January 31, 1983, is referred to as Tyler (ed. Oughton).

[2] For this reason, decided cases under the 1938 and 1965 Acts are relevant and helpful under the new Act: *Re Coventry* [1980] Ch. 461, 474.

[3] For the persons who may apply, see *post*, p. 16. The Law Reform Committee has suggested (Cmnd. 7902) that where a will is revoked by the testator's marriage and at the time of marriage he was incapable the beneficiaries should be entitled to apply to the court for reasonable financial provision if they are persons for whom he might have provided.

under a moral obligation to provide for some members of his "family circle," nevertheless his testamentary freedom is preserved, subject only to the scrutiny of the court that his dispositions should be capable of being regarded as reasonable in all the circumstances.[4]

This discretionary power is the means by which the English Parliament, and the legislatures of the Commonwealth, have sought to solve a set of problems common to all legal systems. These problems may be called the problems of disinheritance, which arise when a testator leaves his property away from his family.

Other legal systems have sought to solve the problems by different means.[5] Some give members of the deceased's family rights to fixed shares of his estate; Scots law gives rights of this kind. Other systems allow family members to claim a fixed share, if they wish. There are numerous variations and combinations. But English law neither specifies what the provision ought to be, nor gives a right to any provision at all; both the right and the *quantum* alike are matters of judicial discretion.

History[6]

In its medieval origins, English law was different; it did give fixed shares. However, the movement towards testamentary freedom was soon under way. The history of the subject is complicated by the distinction between real and personal property, and by differences between different parts of England and Wales. As a great over-simplification, it might be said that there was a large degree of testamentary freedom by about 1400, or at least by 1500, and that testamentary freedom was substantially complete by 1724. However, some limited restrictions lingered until later. The last of them was only removed by section 5 of the Mortmain and Charitable Uses Act 1891. In a sense, therefore, complete testamentary freedom only existed in England for some 47 years, from 1891 to 1938.[7]

By 1938, in fact, the tide of testamentary freedom in the Commonwealth had turned, for a Family Protection Act had been passed in New Zealand in 1908, and some Australian and Canadian jurisdictions had passed similar legislation. In England, the 1938

---

[4] *Re Inns* [1947] Ch. 576, 581; *Re Catmull* [1943] Ch. 262, 268; *Re Joslin* [1941] Ch. 200, 202; *Re Coventry, ante* n. 2; Lord Wilberforce in *Hansard*, H.L. Vol. 358, col. 932.

[5] See the article at (1938) 1 M.L.R. 296; Tyler (ed. Oughton) pp. 1–3.

[6] See Megarry and Wade, *Law of Real Property*, 5th ed., 1984, pp. 539–548; Holdsworth, *History of English Law*, Vol. III, pp. 550–556, Vol. IV, pp. 438, 439, 464–466; Tyler, pp. 3–5; E. S. P. Haynes, *The Lawyer*, p. 219; Tyler (ed. Oughton) gives an especially full treatment of the events leading up to the 1938 Act.

[7] Jarman, *Wills*, 8th ed., p. 74 (Albery).

Act was eventually passed, after persistent advocacy, notably by Eleanor Rathbone M.P. The 1938 Act gave the right to apply for reasonable provision to four classes of persons: wives and husbands; daughters who had not been married, or who were, by reason of mental or physical disability, incapable of maintaining themselves; infant sons; and sons of full age who likewise were, by reason of some mental or physical disability, incapable of maintaining themselves. In its original form, the 1938 Act only applied to the estates of those who left valid wills, but by the Intestates Estates Act 1952 it was extended to the estates of persons who had died intestate. In 1958 separate legislation, the Matrimonial Causes (Property and Maintenance) Act, gave a former spouse who had not remarried the right to apply for reasonable provision; this legislation was later incorporated in the 1965 Act. Next, the Family Provision Act 1966 removed certain restrictions on the powers of the court which had been embodied in the 1938 Act. These successive expansions in the scope of the family provision jurisdiction show how its interference with testamentary freedom became more and more acceptable. Now, after a working paper and a report by the Law Commission,[8] has come the 1975 Act.[9] This lays down a new and comprehensive code, but in the context of the history of the family provision jurisdiction it can be seen as making a jurisdiction which still rests upon the same general basis, the discretionary basis, yet more expansive. It does so in the following five ways:

(a) reasonable provision for a surviving spouse, in contrast to that for other applicants, is such financial provision as it would be reasonable in all the circumstances of the case for a surviving spouse to receive, whether or not the provision is required for his or her maintenance.[10] This change brings such provision closer to that which has to be made following divorce[11];

(b) the number of potential applicants is increased. Persons treated by the deceased as children of the family,[12] and persons who were being wholly or partly maintained by the

---

[8] Law Comm. 61. The extent to which the court can look at this report to help it decide individual cases is uncertain: see *Black-Clawson International Ltd.* v. *Papierwerke Waldhof-Aschaffenburg A.G.* [1975] A.C. 591; *Wachtel* v. *Wachtel* [1973] Fam. 72, 93.

[9] For a brief but useful summary, see Parry and Clarke, *The Law of Succession*, 8th ed., pp. 101–133. The Act is fully and interestingly annotated by J. G. Miller in *Current Law Statutes* (1975). For parliamentary debates see H.L. Deb. Vol. 356, col. 1423; Vol. 358, col. 917; Vol. 361, col. 1377; H.C. Vol. 895, col. 1910.

[10] s. 1(2). Under the 1938 Act the standard of provision for a surviving spouse was restricted to maintenance.

[11] See s. 3(2), and pp. 32–38, *post*.

[12] s. 1(1)(*d*).

deceased at the date of his death,[13] are included. Moreover, such children, and true children of the deceased, may apply whatever their age or marital status;
(c) the powers of the court as to the orders it may make for provision are enlarged[14];
(d) the property available for provision is increased[15];
(e) the court is given the power to interfere with dispositions and contracts intended to defeat applications for family provision.[16]

Themes

A number of general concepts underlay both judicial decisions under, and academic discussion of, the family provision jurisdiction under the 1938 and 1965 Acts. They are likewise proving to do so under the 1975 Act. These concepts are, as it were, themes which with their expositions, developments, and variations make up the law and practice of the subject. They are important practically as well as theoretically, because they must influence almost every judicial decision in a family provision matter to a greater or lesser degree, either explicitly or implicitly. They will be mentioned in particular contexts later, but they can usefully be mentioned generally now.

(a) Maintenance

Applicants other than surviving spouses can apply only for such financial provision as it would be reasonable for them to receive for their maintenance. How far will the court allow this to restrict it from making an order which it would otherwise wish to make, because such other order more nearly gives effect to its concept of what is reasonable provision, although it is less obviously directed to the maintenance of the applicant?

To judge by the decisions on the Act so far, especially the leading case of *Re Coventry*,[17] it appears that the court will treat the maintenance standard as imposing a substantial restriction. "Maintenance" under the 1975 Act means what it meant under the 1938 Act. It is more than just enough to enable a person to get by but does not extend beyond this to include general benefit or welfare.[18]

---

[13] s. 1(1)(e).
[14] s. 2.
[15] ss. 8, 9, 25.
[16] ss. 10,11.
[17] [1980] Ch. 461.
[18] *Re Coventry, supra*; *Re E* [1966] 1 W.L.R. 709; *Millward* v. *Shenton* [1972] 1 W.L.R. 711.

In *Re Christie*[19] the court adopted a different and more generous definition of maintenance in order, in effect, to implement a change in a will which a testatrix had intended but failed to make before she died. This definition of maintenance was disapproved in *Re Coventry*. The disapproval has been generally endorsed.[20] In *Re Dennis*[21] Browne-Wilkinson J. made the following useful observations:

> "The Court has, up until now, declined to define the exact meaning of the word "maintenance' and I am certainly not going to depart from that approach. But in my judgment the word "maintenance' connotes only payments which, directly or indirectly, enable the applicant in the future to discharge the costs of his daily living at whatever standard of living is appropriate to him. The provision that is to be made is to meet recurring expenses, being expenses of living of an income nature. This does not mean that the provision need be by way of income payments. The provision can be by way of a lump sum, for example, to buy a house in which the applicant can be housed, thereby relieving him pro tanto of income expenditure. Nor am I suggesting that there may not be cases in which payment of existing debts may not be appropriate as a maintenance payment; for example, to pay the debts of an applicant in order to enable him to continue to carry on a profit making business or profession may well be for his maintenance."

The learned judge went on to hold that the applicant, an adult son of the deceased, had not shown that he had any arguable prospect of success so as to lead the Court to allow his application to go forward after the 6 month time limit had expired; his claim for a sum of money to pay the capital transfer tax on an *inter vivos* gift made to him by the deceased was not a claim for maintenance.

(b) Dependency

The 1938 Act described the persons entitled to apply under it as "dependants," and the factual relationship of dependency, or the lack of it, could influence the court in making or refusing to make an order.[22] The 1975 Act refers to the persons entitled to apply as "applicants," and they include a separate class of dependants. How

[19] [1979] Ch. 168.
[20] But consider *Re Leach* [1985] 3 W.L.R. 413; *Re Callaghan* [1985] Fam. 1; *post*, p. 42.
[21] [1981] 2 All E.R. 140, 145.
[22] *Re Gregory* [1970] 1 W.L.R. 1455, C.A.

much will the factual relationship of dependency, or the lack of it, still influence the court? It is submitted that where the applicant was being maintained by the deceased in his lifetime, but the entitlement to apply is not based on this fact, the court will be more ready to find that the provision made for the applicant by the will or intestacy was unreasonable. Moreover, the amount of maintenance during the life of the deceased is some guide to the appropriate amount after his death.[23]

(c) Testamentary freedom

In some of the cases under the 1938 Act, the court was influenced by the unqualified freedom of testamentary disposition which had formerly existed in English law.[24] In these cases, the concept of testamentary freedom led the court to refuse to make orders for provision. The new Act works in the same way as the 1938 Act, in so far as it leaves the testator his testamentary freedom, subject only to the discretionary power of the court. The court may attach less importance to testamentary freedom than it did before, though in *Re Coventry*[25] Oliver J. expressly emphasised the Englishman's right (subject to the court's powers under the Act and to fiscal demands) "at his death to dispose of his own property in whatever way he pleases, or, if he chooses to do so, to leave that disposition to be regulated by the laws of intestate succession." Nevertheless, English law may perhaps be moving for good or ill somewhat towards a presumption in favour of at least some of those persons who qualify as applicants under the Act. The change in the standard of reasonable provision for a surviving spouse, from reasonable provision for maintenance to reasonable provision *simpliciter*, may be both an effect of this movement and a cause of further movement in the future.

(d) Family Assets

The idea of family property, so far as it involves the notion that the property of the members of a family belongs in some sense to the family as a whole, is alien to English law. Such at least is the theory. However, for some time now a concept of family assets has influenced discussion and practice in matrimonial property law. The "family assets" are those things which are acquired by one or

---

[23] See also, p. 30, *post*.
[24] *Re Inns* [1947] Ch. 576, 582; *Re Gregory, ante*. It has also been said that there is no prima facie right to provision, and no burden of proof one way or the other: *Re Ducksbury* [1966] 1 W.L.R. 1226.
[25] [1980] Ch. 461, 474.

other or both of the parties to a marriage, with the intention that
they should provide continuing support for them and their children
during their joint lives. The concept first became prominent in cases
on section 17 of the Married Women's Property Act 1882, in which
it was held that the court had power under that section to adjust the
shares of spouses in their family assets. However, the House of
Lords eventually held that there was no such power.[26] Subsequently
the Court of Appeal held that the new powers of financial provision
on divorce given by the Matrimonial Proceedings and Property Act
1970 (and now contained in the Matrimonial Causes Act 1973)
allowed, if indeed they did not oblige, the court to divide the family
assets of the husband and wife undergoing the divorce: see, for
example, the leading case of *Wachtel* v. *Wachtel.*[27] But the use of the
concept has been criticised here too.[28]

There are obvious and intentional[29] similarities between the
discretionary powers of the court under the Matrimonial Causes
Act 1973 and its discretionary powers under the 1975 Act. Perhaps
the concept of family assets will come to be applied in some cases
under the latter Act as it has been under the former. But whether it
is or not, a more general point can be made. The law of family
provision gives a remedy to a member of the deceased's "family
circle" if he or she is unreasonably deprived of provision from the
estate of the deceased. To that extent, the idea of the family
ownership of the family property is already with us.[30] Where there is
a remedy, there is a right.

(e) Moral Obligation

It has been said that the 1938 Act rested on the basis that a deceased
person might be under a moral obligation to provide for surviving
dependants.[31] Much the same could be said of the 1975 Act. The
question why there should be such an obligation is obviously
beyond the scope of discussion here. It is not a legal question at all.
The question why, granted such an obligation, the law should give
effect to it, is a legal question, but it raises general issues of legal and
social policy which will likewise not be considered here, or at least
not at any length. For present purposes, the starting point must be

[26] *Pettitt* v. *Pettitt* [1970] A.C. 777.
[27] [1973] Fam. 72.
[28] *P.* v. *P.* [1978] 1 W.L.R. 483, 487; and see p. 34, *post.*
[29] Law Comm. 61, paras. 16–18, 27.
[30] See the remarks of Bagnall J. in *Harnett* v. *Harnett* [1973] Fam. 156. 160, 161; also, (1980) 10 Fam. Law 141.
[31] Williams and Mortimer, *Executors, Administrators and Probate,* 10th ed., (1970), p. 539; *Re Ducksbury* [1966] 1 W.L.R. 1226.

that Parliament has given legal effect to some sort of moral obligation of this kind. However, one aspect of this moral obligation may usefully be considered. The obligation to provide may derive from a sentiment that family and dependants ought to be left money to live on; or it may derive from a sentiment that they have the primary right to the deceased's property. These sentiments are different, though related, and within the restraints and guidelines provided by the Act and the decided cases they will point the court in divergent directions. The sentiment that family and dependants ought to be left money to live on will point towards a somewhat restrictive exercise of the jurisdiction, emphasising the concept of maintenance. The sentiment that family and dependants have the primary right to the deceased's property will point towards a generous exercise of the jurisdiction, and towards ideas of family property.

(f) The Limits of the Obligation

The obligation discussed in the preceding section is one of those "underlying principles which most rubrics of the law disclose, almost invariably so general as to be incapable of precise definition."[32] However, under the 1938 Act the limits of the obligation were marked out by three boundary features, as it were. First, the obligation was an obligation to maintain only. Secondly, it was limited to persons who were linked to the deceased by ties of marriage or parenthood. Thirdly, those persons were likely to be dependent upon the deceased as a matter of fact. The successive amendments to the 1938 Act, and the introduction of similar legislation relating to former spouses, did not remove these boundary features.

The 1975 Act partly removed them. The removal of the maintenance standard of provision for spouses raises rather special considerations, which will be considered later.[33] The grant of the right to apply to adult children, to children of the family, and to persons maintained by the deceased, has a more general significance. The Act gives no definite guidance as to how far and how readily the Courts ought to travel beyond the old boundaries, and make orders in favour of adult children, children of the family, and persons maintained by the deceased. Three different degrees of adventurousness, as it were, are possible for the Court on the mere language of the Act, and all three have been adopted in the reported cases. Most cautiously, the Court can refuse to travel beyond the old

---

[32] Goff and Jones, *The Law of Restitution*, 2nd ed., p. 11.
[33] See pp. 32 *et seq. post.*

boundaries, unless there is some special factor or circumstance which spurs it to do so. Rather more adventurously, the Court can pass beyond the old boundary features not only if there is some special factor or circumstance, but also if the facts before it are analogous to, but not the same as, facts which would have given the applicant rights before the 1975 Act was passed, either under the old family provision legislation or under some principles of law or equity. Most adventurously, and indeed rashly, the Court can be so willing to favour an application by another child, child of the family, or person maintained by the deceased as to come closer and closer to replacing the terms of the will or the rules of intestacy by its own general ideas of fairness in the particular case.

The most cautious approach is that of Oliver J. (as he then was) in *Re Coventry*.[34] The second, somewhat more adventurous approach is the one which pays regard to analogies between *de facto* relationships and the legal relationships of husband and wife and parent and child, as in *Re McC, CA* v. *CC*.[35] It can also be seen, perhaps, in the way in which the reliance upon the deceased of a person maintained by him can be likened to the reliance which works an estoppel; this is hinted at by Stephenson L.J. in *Jelley* v. *Iliffe*.[36] The third and most adventurous approach is the one adopted in *Re Christie*,[37] and subsequently much criticised, although two later cases on applications by children of the family, *Re Callaghan*[38] and *Re Leach*[39] shows signs of its persistence.

It is submitted that the most cautious approach is the correct one, although the second approach, with its reliance on analogies, can also be appropriate and helpful in some cases. The third and most adventurous approach is simply wrong[40].

---

[34] [1980] Ch. 461; [1979] C.L.J. 286.
[35] "The Times," November 11, 1978; (1979) 9 Fam. Law 26; (1979) 123 Sol. Jo. 35.
[36] [1981] Fam. 128; and see p. 24, *post.*
[37] [1979] Ch. 168; [1979] C.L.J. 286.
[38] [1984] 3 W.L.R. 1076.
[39] [1984] Fam. Law 24.
[40] *Re Coventry, Supra; Re Homer, Rann* v. *Jackson*, C.A., November 16, 1978, C.A.T. 78/723; Tyler (ed. Oughton) pp. 41–43; [1985] Conv. 258 (a discussion of the recent working of the Act).

2 Preliminary Requirements

Certain requirements must be satisfied before the court has jurisdiction and can exercise its powers under the 1975 Act.

Date of Death

The deceased must have died after the commencement of the Act.[1] The Act came into force on April 1, 1976.[2] Therefore, the deceased must have died after the moment of midnight between March 31 and April 1, 1976.

Domicile

The deceased must have died domiciled in England and Wales.[3] In English law, a person's domicile is his permanent home, as the law understands it.[4] The burden of establishing that the deceased died domiciled in England and Wales lies on the applicant for provision,[5] although if the point is not disputed the statement to that effect in the probate or letters of administration ought to be sufficient evidence.

The requirement that the deceased must have died domiciled in England has been criticised.[6] The critics have suggested that the normal rule of English private international law ought to apply, whereby succession to movables is governed by the law of the last domicile of the deceased, and succession to immovables by the law of the place where the immovables are situate. On the other hand, the requirement has been defended on the ground that the question whether the surviving members of a deceased person's family should have a claim to an interest in his estate should be governed by his personal law, which is the law of his domicile.[7] Either basis of

---

[1] s. 1(1). If he or she died before, the 1938 and 1965 Acts apply: see s. 26.
[2] s. 27.
[3] s. 1(1).
[4] For domicile, see Dicey and Morris, *Conflict of Laws*, 10th ed., 1980, pp. 100–148.
[5] *Mastaka* v. *Midland Bank Executor and Trustee Co. Ltd.* [1941] Ch. 192; *Re Harmsworth* [1982] C.L.Y. 3388.
[6] See Tyler (ed. Oughton) p. 46.
[7] Law Comm. 61, para. 262.

jurisdiction could produce anomalies, and there seems much to be said for the view of the Law Commission that the point is best left to be resolved by an international convention.

Time for Application

Section 4 of the Act provides that an application for an order shall not, except with the permission of the court,[8] be made after the end of the period of six months from the date on which representation with respect to the estate of the deceased is first taken out. In considering when representation with respect to an estate was first taken out, a grant limited to settled land or to trust property is to be left out of account, and so is a grant limited to real estate or to personal estate unless a grant limited to the remainder of the estate has previously been made or is made at the same time.[9]

Under the 1938 Act, if a will which had already been proved in common form was subsequently proved in solemn form, a fresh period of six months did not start to run with the proof in solemn form, because such proof merely affirmed the original grant in common form.[10] But if one will was proved and another will was later discovered and proved, the six month period probably ran only from the date of proof of the later will.[11] There is now authority to this effect. In *Re Freeman*[12] a grant in common form had been revoked because the execution of the will was shown not to have been properly attested. The Court held that "representation" in section 4 means "effective" or "valid" representation, so that the six month period ran from the later grant. That later grant was in fact a grant of letters of administration on intestacy, but the principle must be the same whatever the nature of the later grant.

The existence of a grant is not a precondition of an application; an application can be made before grant.[13] It is suggested that the executors named in the unproved will, or the beneficiaries if different, should be made defendants. There will have to be a grant at a later stage, if an order is to be made. Should there be no person both entitled and willing to take out a grant, the Official Solicitor may be prepared to do so, in order to enable the claim to go forward. A grant to the Official Solicitor may also be appropriate

---

[8] The extension of time cannot affect joint property: s. 9.
[9] s. 23. It is submitted that, by analogy, other limited grants, for example those *ad colligenda bona* or *pendente lite*, do not count either. *Cf. Re Bidie* [1949] Ch. 121.
[10] *Re Miller* [1969] 1 W.L.R. 583.
[11] *Re Bidie* [1949] Ch. 121.
[12] [1984] 1 W.L.R. 1419.
[13] *Re Searle* [1949] Ch. 73.

when the applicant is the person primarily entitled to a grant, and no one else is entitled and willing to take it out.[14] Applicants can protect themselves from being caught unawares by a grant by making use of the new "standing search" procedure.[15] Personal representatives are protected if they distribute the estate of the deceased after the end of the six-month period, although this does not prejudice any power to recover any part of the estate so distributed.[16] The powers referred to are presumably the powers, if any, available to recover assets wrongly paid under the principles relating to refunding and tracing.[17] Before the six–month period has expired, personal representatives distribute the estate at their own risk, and they ought to be prepared to resist any pressure by the beneficiaries to make anticipatory payments. However, they should not adopt a purely negative attitude. In *Re Ralphs*[18] Cross J., as he then was, after consultation with his fellow judges of the Chancery Division, gave guidance which is as useful under the 1975 Act as it was under the 1938 Act. He said that personal representatives: "should form their own view, with the assistance, of course, of their legal advisers, as to the payments which can properly be made, and if they are not prepared to make such payments on their own responsibility, they should ask the parties who might conceivably be affected, whether applicant or residuary legatee, for their consent. If such consent is not forthcoming the executors can apply to the court for leave to make the payment in question, and the court, if it thinks that any withholding of consent was unreasonable, could throw the costs of the application on the party to blame."

The circumstances in which personal representatives can safely make payments are difficult to define precisely, but it is thought that there could be little injury to the estate (or danger to the personal representatives) in paying, to an applicant who was given a benefit by the will and is asking for more, his entitlement under the will; or in paying his legacy to a legatee whose legacy is trifling in comparison with the size of the residue; or in paying his legacy to a legatee who has a high moral claim and is suffering hardship for want of money.[19]

---

[14] See also Williams, Mortimer and Sunnucks, p. 322.
[15] Williams, Mortimer and Sunnucks, p. 348. The *caveat* procedure is not appropriate.
[16] s. 20(1). On the wording of the section, personal representatives would not appear to be protected if they distribute any part of the estate after proceedings have actually been commenced.
[17] See Williams, Mortimer and Sunnucks, p. 970; Goff and Jones, *The Law of Restitution* 2nd ed., pp. 46–63.
[18] [1968] 1 W.L.R. 1522.
[19] See *Re Ralphs, ante.*

Extension of Time

Under the 1975 Act, the court's discretion to extend the six-month time limit for applications is unfettered, as it eventually was under the 1938 Act, after its amendment by the Family Provision Act 1966.[20] In *Re Ruttie*,[21] Ungoed-Thomas J. rejected the suggestion that the discretion should be exercised with the same indulgence as is exercised towards procedural time limits, where extension is granted except "when irreparable mischief would be done by acceding to a tardy application," but he considered that it would be premature to lay down any alternative guiding principles. Under the 1975 Act courts of first instance have identified some guidelines. In *Re Salmon*[22] Megarry J. set out six considerations, "plainly not exhaustive," which should guide the court in the exercise of its discretion:

(1) The discretion is unfettered, and is thus to be exercised judicially and in accordance with what is just and proper.

(2) The onus is on the plaintiff to establish sufficient grounds for the case to be taken out of the general rule, thus depriving those who are protected by it of its benefits.

(3) It is material to consider how promptly and in what circumstances the applicant seeks the permission of the court after the time limit has expired. The whole of the circumstances have to be looked at,[23] and not least the reasons for the delay, and the promptitude with which, by letter before action or otherwise, the claimant gives warning to the defendants of the proposed application. Where there has been some error or oversight, an obvious question is whether the applicant has done all that is reasonably possible to put matters right promptly, and has kept the defendants informed.

(4) It is obviously material whether or not negotiations have been commenced within the time limit; even negotiations commenced after the time limit may aid the applicant.

(5) It is also relevant to consider whether or not the estate has been distributed before a claim under the Act has been made or notified.

(6) It is relevant to consider whether a refusal to extend the time would leave the claimant without redress against his advisers.

---

[20] Where an extension is sought, this relief should be expressly asked for in the originating summons, and the grounds on which it is claimed should be set out in the affidavit in support: *Practice Note* [1976] 1 W.L.R. 418.

[21] [1970] 1 W.L.R. 89.

[22] [1981] Ch. 167.

[23] Including any representation made by a beneficiary: *Re John* (1967) 111 S.J. 15.

These guidelines are not exhaustive, and a further aid to the court is to consider whether the applicant has an arguable case by reference to the same factors as are considered when deciding whether to give leave to defend under Order 14 of the Rules of the Supreme Court.[24] The existence of a pending application by another applicant is presumably also relevant.[25]

In the two cases[26] on extension of time which have reached the Court of Appeal, that Court has not disputed the usefulness of the various guidelines. However, it has tended to emphasise the unfettered nature of the discretion, and the decision in *Re Adams* substantially reduces the significance of the sixth guideline in *Re Salmon*. Ormrod L.J. said that "it seems to me that the right approach is to consider the justice of the case as between the parties, first of all, and to take into account all the matters set out very helpfully by the Vice Chancellor in *Re Salmon*. It is only if, having done that computation, one finds that the plaintiff on the one hand has suffered severe prejudice, and the defendant on the other hand has suffered severe prejudice, or will if the limitation period is extended, that the claim for damages against the plaintiff's solicitors becomes relevant." Dunn L.J. simply remarked that "Speaking for myself, I am not prepared to go so far as to say that the chance of the plaintiff having a remedy against his or her solicitors is a wholly irrelevant consideration under section 4."

Failure to make Reasonable Provision

The preliminary requirements already discussed are preconditions of jurisdiction to consider an application at all. Failure to make reasonable provision is a precondition of an order. The court has to proceed in two stages.[27] First it must be satisfied that the disposition of the deceased's estate is not such as to make reasonable financial provision. Secondly, if it is so satisfied, it may itself make reasonable provision.[28] The matters to which the court is directed to have regard at both stages are the same, but the result of considering them may be different, in the sense that, at the first stage, the court may decide that the disposition of the deceased's estate does make reasonable provision, and therefore may not proceed to the second

---

[24] *Re Stone* (1969) 114 S.J. 36; *Re Dennis* [1981] 2 All E.R. 140.

[25] See *post*, p. 52 for the relationship between s. 4 and s. 6 (Variation of Orders).

[26] *Re Adams*, C.A., July 22, 1981, C.A.T. 81/299; *Re Escritt*, C.A., October 15, 1981, C.A.T. 81/396.

[27] *Re Singer* [1967] 1 W.L.R. 1482, 1486, 1487; *Re Coventry* [1980] Ch. 461, 469; *See* (1984) 14 Fam. Law 171 for a comment.

[28] s. 3(1). Note that provision which is reasonable in amount may be unreasonable because of a condition to which it is subject: *Re Doring* [1955] 1 W.L.R. 1217.

stage, although, if it had proceeded to the second stage, it would have made somewhat different provision itself. Reasonable provision is an area rather than a point.[29] The two stages must be kept separate because the Act envisages them as separate.[30] At the first stage, the test of whether reasonable provision has been made is objective. The question is not whether the deceased was reasonable in making the provision he did, but whether the provision actually made is reasonable. The objective nature of the test appears from the wording of the Act,[31] and is consonant with the interpretation of the test under the 1938 Act which eventually achieved general acceptance.[32]

Consistently with the objective nature of the test, the court must take into account the facts as known to it at the date of the hearing.[33]

An objective test is the only one which can be applied when an applicant alleges that the disposition of the deceased's estate effected by the law relating to intestacy fails to make reasonable provision for him or her. The effect of the intestacy rules cannot be reasonable or unreasonable in a subjective sense. At first sight, it might appear strange that rules laid down, as the intestacy rules are, for the purpose of making reasonable provision, should need to be subject to a dispensing power in case they do not do so.[34] The reason is of course that general rules are inflexible and cannot produce the correct result in every case. For example, the extensive rights given to widows and widowers on intestacy operate for the best in the great majority of instances, but they can produce an unreasonable result sometimes. One instance is where the marriage to the widow or widower was a second or subsequent marriage, and the deceased left dependent children by an earlier marriage.

[29] Jarman *Wills*, 8th ed., p. 79 (Albery).
[30] See the opening of s. 3(1).
[31] See the concluding words of s. 1(1).
[32] *Millward* v. *Shenton* [1972] 1 W.L.R. 711.
[33] s. 3(5).
[34] For cases under the former legislation where the deceased died intestate, see *Re Cook* [1956] 106 L.J. 466; *Re Singer* [1967] 1 W.L.R. 1482; *Re Trowell* [1957] C.L.Y. 3745. For cases under the 1975 Act, see *Re Coventry, supra; Re Kozdrach* [1981] Conv. 224; *Re Kirby* (1981) 11 Fam. Law 210; *Re Wood* (1982) 79 L.S. Gaz. 774; *Harrington* v. *Gill* (1983) 4 F.L.R. 265; *Re Callaghan* [1985] Fam. 1; *Re Leach* [1985] 3 W.L.R. 413.

3 Persons Entitled to Apply

The 1975 Act allows any of the following persons to apply for provision[1]:

(a) the wife[2] or husband of the deceased;

(b) a former wife or former husband of the deceased who has not remarried;

(c) a child of the deceased;

(d) any person (not being a child of the deceased) who, in the case of any marriage to which the deceased was at any time a party, was treated by the deceased as a child of the family in relation to that marriage;

(e) any person (not being a person included in the foregoing categories) who immediately before the death of the deceased was being maintained, either wholly or partly, by the deceased.

Presumably an applicant's right to apply comes to an end on his or her death, because section 2 of the Act refers to orders being made for provision to or for the benefit of the applicant.[3] If the right to apply does survive for the benefit of the estate of an applicant other than a spouse, it is hard to see how any order could properly be made in the exercise of the court's discretion, except possibly one which provided maintenance for the period between the death of the deceased and the death of the applicant. However, if the right survives for the benefit of the estate of an applicant spouse, a more generous order could be made. This distinction is the result of the different meanings of "reasonable financial provision" in section 1(2) of the Act.

There is nothing to prevent a bankrupt from applying, but he is

---

[1] s. 1(1).

[2] A wife bears the burden of proving her marriage to the deceased, so should in strictness adduce evidence of it, and should certainly do so if it may be disputed: *Re Peete* [1952] 2 All E.R. 599; *Re Watkins* [1953] 1 W.L.R. 1323. By analogy all other applicants must likewise bear the burden of proving their membership of the relevant category: *Re Wilkinson* [1978] Fam. 22; *Re Beaumont* [1980] Ch. 444.

[3] This is the law for applications for financial provision under the Matrimonial Jurisdiction: *D'Este* v. *D'Este* [1973] Fam. 55.

unlikely to succeed and any lump sum award will vest in his trustee, and any award of periodical payments may be gathered in by the trustee.[4]

At common law, the rule which precluded a person who had unlawfully killed another from acquiring a benefit in consequence of the killing also precluded him from applying for provision out of that other's estate under the family provision jurisdiction.[5] As a result of sections 3 and 5 of the Forfeiture Act 1982, it is only persons convicted of murder who are so precluded.

A Wife or Husband

This surviving spouse category includes a person who in good faith entered into a void marriage with the deceased, unless either (a) the marriage was dissolved or annulled during the lifetime of the deceased and the dissolution or annulment is recognised by the law of England and Wales, or (b) that person has during the lifetime of the deceased entered into a later marriage.[6] As a result of this definition, there could be more than one surviving spouse entitled to claim provision as the wife or husband of a deceased person, if the void marriage had been followed by a further marriage. The same could happen as a result of a polygamous marriage.[7] These unusual situations need create no insuperable problems because, as will be seen when the matters to be considered by the court are discussed, the provision which it is reasonable for an applicant to receive will vary with the number and weight of the claims to provision possessed by other applicants and by the existing beneficiaries under the Will or intestacy of the deceased.[8]

There is no reason why an application by a widower should be less favourably entertained than one by a widow, merely because the applicant is a widower. Early cases[9] to that effect under the 1938 Act were subsequently disapproved,[10] and the disapproval must still operate. Widowers may well apply less often than widows, and perhaps succeed less often, but that will be because they are usually more able to support themselves. It will not be merely because they are widowers.

---

[4] Under ss. 38(a) and 51(2) of the Bankruptcy Act 1914, respectively. See the Australian Case of *Coffey* v. *Bennett* [1961] V.R. 264. The power to settle property could be used to assist a bankrupt and his family. See p. 49, *post.*
[5] *Re Royse* [1984] 3 W.L.R. 784.
[6] s. 25(4). For the meaning of "remarriage," see s. 25(5).
[7] Law Comm. 61, para. 29; *Re Sehota* [1978] 1 W.L.R. 1506.
[8] See p. 27, *post.*
[9] *Re Sylvester* [1941] Ch. 87; *Re Styler* [1942] Ch. 387.
[10] *Re Clayton* [1966] 1 W.L.R. 969, 972.

The remarriage of a surviving spouse does not automatically terminate an order for periodical payments under the Act, although it may provide a ground for varying it.[11]

The general standard of reasonable provision for a surviving spouse is such provision as it would be reasonable in all the circumstances of the case for the surviving spouse to receive, whether or not that provision is required for his or her maintenance.[12] However, if the marriage was the subject of a decree of judicial separation and at the date of death the decree was in force and the separation continuing, it is such provision as would be reasonable for maintenance.

A Former Wife or Former Husband

This is the former spouse category. "Former wife" or "former husband" means a person whose marriage with the deceased was during the deceased's lifetime dissolved or annulled by a decree under the Matrimonial Causes Act 1973.[13] Persons whose marriages were dissolved abroad have now the same rights to apply for provision under the 1975 Act as persons whose marriages are dissolved or annulled under the 1973 Act.[14]

The general standard of reasonable provision for former spouses is such provision as would be reasonable for maintenance.[15] A former spouse will usually have had the opportunity to apply for more under the matrimonial jurisdiction at the time of the divorce or annulment, so the restriction to reasonable provision for maintenance is sensible.[16] However, it could operate unfairly if the death of one spouse followed soon after the divorce or annulment, so that the surviving former spouse had no opportunity of obtaining an order under the matrimonial jurisdiction. For this reason, the Act provides[17] that where within 12 months from the date on which a decree of divorce or nullity has been made absolute or a decree of judicial separation has been granted, a party to the marriage dies and either (a) an application for financial provision or for property

---

[11] This follows from the terms of s. 2(1), s. 19(2) and s. 6(3); *cf.* orders made in favour of former spouses and judicially separated spouses.

[12] s. 1(2); and see pp. 32–38, *post.*

[13] s. 25(1).

[14] s. 25(1) of the 1975 Act has been amended by s. 25 of the Matrimonial and Family Proceedings Act 1984 which provides that a surviving former spouse whose marriage was dissolved or annulled outside England and Wales may make a claim for reasonable financial provision from the estate of the deceased former spouse under the 1975 Act as amended by s. 8 of the 1984 Act.

[15] s. 1(2).

[16] Law Comm. 61, para. 19 onwards; *Re Fullard* [1982] Fam. 42.

[17] s. 14.

adjustment under the Matrimonial Causes Act 1973 has not been made by the surviving party, or (b) such an application has been made but the proceedings have not been determined at the time of the death of the deceased party, then, if an application under section 2 of the Act is made, the court shall have the power to treat the surviving party as if there had been no decree of divorce, nullity, or judicial separation. Therefore, financial provision can be awarded on the more generous basis, disregarding the maintenance restriction. The power only exists in a case of judicial separation if at the death of the deceased the decree of judicial separation was still in force and the separation continuing;[18] if it is not, then the maintenance restriction does not apply anyway.[19]

Four special provisions of the Act relating to the rights of former spouses should be noted. First, in matrimonial proceeedings the court is empowered, on the application of either party to the marriage, to bar future applications for family provision.[20] This provides a means whereby property arrangements on the break up of a marriage can be given the advantage of finality. Secondly, on an application under the Act by a person entitled to payments from the deceased under a secured periodical payments order made under the Matrimonial Causes Act 1973, the court is given power to vary or discharge that order.[21] Thirdly, the court has a similar power to vary or revoke a maintenance agreement, on an application under the Act by a person entitled to payments under such an agreement.[22] Fourthly, the reverse applies: where an application is made under section 31(6) of the Matrimonial Causes Act 1973 for the variation or discharge of a secured periodical payments order after the death of the payer, or under section 36(1) of the Matrimonial Causes Act 1973 for the alteration of a maintenance agreement, the court has power, in effect, to treat the application as an application under the Act and exercise its powers thereunder.[23] This does not apply, however, if future applications under the Act have been barred by an order under section 15 of the Act, as explained above.

[18] s. 14(2).
[19] Anecdotal evidence received by the author suggests that the 12 month period may be too short.
[20] s. 15, as amended by s. 8 of the Matrimonial and Family Proceedings Act 1984; the consent of both parties was required under the original s. 15. Law Comm. 61, paras. 185–188. Apart from this provision, it is submitted that public policy prevents "contracting out" of the Act. This was the law under the 1965 Act (*Re M.* [1968] P. 174), although there was no decision under the 1938 Act.
[21] s. 16; Law Comm. 61, paras. 263–276.
[22] s. 17.
[23] s. 18.

A Child of the Deceased

This includes an illegitimate child, and a child *en ventre sa mère* on the death of the deceased.[24] In contrast to the 1938 Act, there is no distinction between sons and daughters, and neither age nor marriage automatically disqualifies a child of either sex as an applicant. Age and marital status are matters which the court will consider,[25] but they are not automatic bars.[26] In this respect it is submitted that the 1975 Act is right.

However, it could be argued that the same cannot be said of the restriction of the standard of provision for children to reasonable provision for maintenance. It could be said that in appropriate cases children look to their parents not only for their maintenance, but also for their "advancement," as that word is legally understood, that is some payment of a capital nature, or at least a non-recurring nature, which is made to establish a child in life. One obvious example of an advancement is a deposit on a house. It could be argued that the law of family provision should recognise this expectation by making the standard of provision for children extend to advancement as well as maintenance,[27] especially now that there is no age limit for a child applicant. Only time will tell whether the court will interpret maintenance broadly, so as to extend it to payments which could be characterised as advancements, or whether it will refuse to order payment for such things as the deposit on a house on the ground that they are not maintenance. It is submitted that the court should and could interpret maintenance quite broadly, so as to allow it to order payments for such purposes if it considers them otherwise appropriate in the particular case. The court could justify such payments on the ground that they are in a sense capitalised maintenance.[28] For example, the deposit on a house helps to provide an applicant with somewhere to live, which is an essential part of maintenance.[29] This broad view of maintenance finds support in the Act itself, by reason of the wide range of orders which the court can make in favour of all applicants, and not

[24] s. 25. Also an adopted child, by virtue of the general provisions of the Adoption Acts.
[25] *Re Coventry* [1980] Ch. 461; *Re Homer, Rann* v. *Jackson*, C.A., 15th November, 1978, C.A.T. 78/723.
[26] If a young child may need provision when he or she is older, the proceedings can be adjourned: *Re Franks* [1948] Ch. 62; and see p. 53, *post*.
[27] Compare, for example, the Testator's Family Maintenance and Guardianship of Infants Act 1916–1954 of New South Wales—"maintenance, education, or advancement in life."
[28] In this way the court could, if it felt it necessary, avoid the disapproval of orders for legacies expressed in cases under the 1938 Act such as *Re Vrint* [1940] Ch. 920 and *Re Clayton* [1966] 1 W.L.R. 969.
[29] See the passage from *Re Dennis* [1981] 2 All E.R. 140, 145, cited *supra*, p. 5.

just surviving spouses. Several of these possible orders[30] are more appropriate for making what is in effect capital provision—"advancement" in the case of a child—rather than maintenance in any narrow sense.

It is submitted that *Re Coventry*[31] is not an insuperable obstacle to this interpretation of maintenance being adopted in an appropriate case. However, it is an indication that the court will be reluctant to adopt such an interpretation unless the circumstances of the case before it otherwise favour the making of an order. *Re Callaghan*[32] and *Re Leach*[33] could be said to be examples of this interpretation of maintenance being adopted where there were such circumstances. Another example might be one in which the estate is substantial and can afford to make provision of the kind referred to without any hardship to the beneficiaries.

If an order for periodical payments is made in favour of a child applicant, the order may provide for the payments to be made to the child's mother, on her undertaking to maintain the child.[34]

A Person Treated by the Deceased as a Child of the Family

This is a new category. The concept of a "child of the family" is imported from the matrimonial law.[35] As a member of the family circle of the deceased, a child of the family who was not a natural or adopted child of the deceased is thought of as having claims upon the deceased, just as his natural or adopted children have. As with natural or adopted children, the maintenance standard of provision applies.[36]

The relevant treatment of the applicant can include events which precede or follow the period of the marriage.[37]

In deciding whether reasonable provision has been made for a person treated as a child of the family, and in deciding what provision ought to be made, the court is directed[38] to have regard:

(a) to whether the deceased had assumed any responsibility for the child's maintenance and, if so, to the extent to which and

---

[30] For example, the power to order a transfer of property.
[31] [1980] Ch. 461.
[32] [1985] Fam. 1.
[33] [1984] 3 W.L.R. 413.
[34] *Re Westby* [1946] W.N. 141; see also n. 33, *post*, p. 51.
[35] Matrimonial Causes Act 1973, s. 52(1), although under that Act the child must have been treated as a child of the family by both parties to the marriage.
[36] s. 1(2).
[37] *Re Leach*, supra; and see p. 42, *post*.
[38] s. 3(3). Compare the Matrimonial Causes Act 1973, s. 25(3).

the basis upon which the deceased assumed that responsibility, and to the length of time for which the deceased discharged that responsibility;

(b) to whether in assuming and discharging that responsibility the deceased did so knowing that the child was not his own child; and

(c) to the liability of any other person to maintain the child.

A Person Maintained by the Deceased

This is another new category, made up of persons who are only entitled to apply for provision because they were being maintained by the deceased immediately before his death. The word "immediately" refers not simply to the moment of death, but to the settled basis or arrangement between the parties at that moment.[39]

The Act provides that a person shall be treated as being maintained by the deceased, either wholly or partly, if the deceased, otherwise than for full valuable consideration, was making a substantial contribution in money or money's worth towards the reasonable needs of that person.[40] The applicant must establish, first, that the deceased was making a substantial contribution in money or money's worth towards the reasonable needs of the applicant, and secondly, that the deceased was so doing otherwise than for full valuable consideration.[41] The reference to "full valuable consideration" was not merely intended to exclude maintenance provided under a contract.[42]

The category is a very wide one. It covers both relatives by blood or marriage other than those already qualified to apply for provision, and also other persons whose sole tie with the deceased was the factual relationship of maintenance. It can include an elderly housekeeper[43] who receives food, shelter, warmth and

[39] *Re Beaumont* [1980] Ch. 444, 482; *Jelley* v. *Iliffe* [1981] Fam. 128; *Kourkey* v. *Lusher* (1982) 12 Fam. Law 86, In *Re Dymott*, C.A. December 15, 1980, C.A.T. 80/942 Ormrod L.J. spoke of "the norm of this relationship" being one of no dependency.

[40] s. 1(3); the subsection is a restrictive provision, and as a matter of grammar ought perhaps be read with the word "only" before the word "if": *Re Beaumont, supra* at p. 451.

[41] *Re Wilkinson* [1978] Fam. 22. The provision of accommodation may be a substantial contribution to needs: *Jelley* v. *Iliffe, ante.*

[42] *Re Beaumont, supra*; *Jelley* v. *Iliffe, ante*; (1978) 94 L.Q.R. 175; (1978) 41 M.L.R. 352.

[43] It was held under the 1938 Act that a deceased person did not owe a moral obligation to his housekeeper merely because she was such: *Re Preston* [1969] 1 W.L.R. 317. But this does not affect the right of a housekeeper to apply for provision as a person maintained by the deceased (if she was such) under the 1975 Act.

clothing in return for purely nominal services; a nephew who is attending school at the expense of the deceased; and a widowed sister who is receiving board and lodging in the home of the deceased but making some contribution in cash to the expenses of the home.[44] It can also include a lover or a mistress, whether fairly describable as a *"de facto* spouse" or not.[45] In an appropriate case, a parent could apply, and so could a grandparent or (perhaps more likely) a grandchild. So could a former spouse who had remarried, in the most unlikely event of her still being maintained by the deceased.

At first sight, the idea underlying this category of applicant might seem to be that the maintaining of a person by the deceased during his life may have put him under an obligation to continue the maintenance after his death. This is consistent with the guideline in the Act[46] that, in considering whether reasonable financial provision has been made for an applicant in this category, and in deciding what provision (if any) to order, the Court must have regard to the extent to which, and the basis upon which, the deceased assumed responsibility for the maintenance of the applicant, and to the length of time for which he or she discharged that responsibility.

Despite the potentially restrictive effect of this guideline, the category remains a wide one. It may be thought that the mere maintenance of one person by another while both are alive creates no obligation on the person providing the maintenance to continue it after his death. Moreover, it may be suspected that Parliament did not intend to recognise any such wide obligation, and that no one else thought that Parliament ought to or was recognising it. These suspicions are justified. The Law Commission Report and the discussion and comment preceding the 1975 Act, and also the way in which the Courts have applied the Act and the discussion and comment on its application, strongly suggest that the category is an umbrella, intended to cover three situations which are often related in fact, but are logically distinct.

The first situation is one of accidental or unintentional failure to make provision. As the Law Commission Report expressed it, "... where a deceased person was contributing to someone's maintenance before his death his failure to make provision for that person may have been accidental or unintentional; he may have

---

[44] Law Comm. 61, para. 98; see further p. 42. For claims by sisters, see *Re Wilkinson, ante,* and *Re Viner* [1978] C.L.Y. 3091.

[45] A lover or mistress is not necessarily a *"de facto* spouse"; in *Malone* v. *Harrison* [1979] 1 W.L.R. 1353 the deceased had both a *"de facto* spouse" and a mistress, the mistress being the applicant.

[46] s. 3(4); This is the only particular guideline for applicants under section 1(1)(e); see p. 42, *post.*

made no will; his will may be stale; or his will may have operated in a way he did not anticipate (for example, the specific legacies may exhaust the estate and leave no residue). In these cases an order for family provision would be doing for the deceased what he might reasonably be assumed to have wished to do himself. This argument carries particular weight where the "dependant" is a person with whom the deceased has been cohabiting."[47]

The second situation is one in which the Act is required to remedy "the injustice of one, who has been put by a deceased person in a position of dependency upon him, being deprived of any financial support, either by accident or by design of the deceased, after his death," as Stephenson L.J. said in *Jelley* v. *Iliffe*.[48] Since the applicant presumably did not have to accept the maintenance when it was offered to him, unless perhaps the circumstances were very special, the words of the learned Lord Justice seem to suggest a kind of quasi-estoppel, or at least an idea related to estoppel. The applicant has changed his position as a result of his continuing receipt of maintenance, so that it would be unreasonable for him to be deprived of it.

The third situation exists when the relationship between the deceased and the applicant was similar to the relationship which would have existed between the deceased and a spouse or child of his. The paramount example here is the "*de facto* spouse."

All these three situations are capable of coming within the category, but in some cases they may not do so. For example, a "*de facto* spouse" who was self supporting or who made a contribution to the joint income which was the same as or greater than that of the deceased is not qualified to apply under the Act, however deserving on other grounds her moral claim to provision may be. On the other hand, a person whose moral claim upon the deceased's bounty may have been much less is qualified to claim if there was maintenance. For example, a woman who was maintained by the deceased in a relationship which had no similarity to marriage is qualified to apply.

Odd results could follow in other cases too. Suppose three elderly ladies make their home together, pooling their respective incomes in proportion, to some extent, to the size of those incomes. One owns the house in which the three of them live, but has no more income than the state pension. The second has, in addition to her state pension, a substantial private pension or income from investments. The third has no more than the state pension. Because of the pooling arrangement, the first and second ladies are not maintain-

---

[47] Law Comm. 61, para. 90.
[48] *Ante*, at 137, 138. Law Comm. 61, para. 88.

(f) any physical or mental disability of any applicant for an order or any beneficiary[2] of the estate of the deceased;

(g) any other matter, including the conduct of the applicant or any other person, which in the circumstances of the case the court may consider relevant.

It will be seen that the guidelines are vague, and open ended. Indeed, the statement that the court is to have regard to any other matter which in the circumstances of the case it may consider relevant is almost an invitation to the court to make its own additional guidelines, both in individual cases and also generally.[3] The guidelines resemble those laid down by statute for financial provision in the matrimonial jurisdiction,[4] and also those set out in the 1938 Act and developed by the court under it. This is not surprising because all three sets of guidelines are very much matters of commonsense and are concerned with a somewhat similar type of problem.

The Balancing of Claims

The first four of the general guidelines are balancing guidelines. The court has to balance the competing claims of applicants and beneficiaries by reference to their different resources and needs, and the obligations and responsibilities owed by the deceased to each of them. The first four guidelines render statutory a judicial method that was explicit[5] or implicit in many if not most cases under the 1938 Act, for under that Act large provision, small provision, or no provision at all was likewise the result of this balancing of conflicting claims by reference to the resources and needs of applicants and beneficiaries and the obligations owed to them by the deceased. Lying behind all this is, perhaps, an older image of the reasonable testator, who makes reasonable provision for the persons

---

[2] Including a beneficiary under a statutory nomination or a *donatio mortis causa*: s. 25(1).

[3] Note the way in which the Court of Appeal laid down additional guidelines for the matrimonial jurisdiction in *Wachtel* v. *Wachtel* [1973] Fam. 72. In both the matrimonial jurisdiction and the family provision jurisdiction, Parliament has granted the Courts great powers over the property of individual citizens, exercisable in accordance with guidelines expressed in very general terms. It is perhaps surprising that this has not given rise to criticism on grounds of constitutional propriety.

[4] Matrimonial Causes Act 1973, s. 25(1).

[5] *Re Joslin* [1941] Ch. 200; *Re E.* [1966] 1 W.L.R. 709; *Re Clarke* [1968] 1 W.L.R. 415. Also under the 1965 Act: *Re Eyre* [1968] 1 W.L.R. 530, and the cases there cited.

who have claims upon his bounty by weighing up their respective resources and his obligations to them.[6]

However, the criticism can be made that the Act gives too little guidance on the weight of the competing claims, and of the different guidelines. For example, the Act gives no indication of the direction in which the Court should move when one party has the greater need, but the deceased owed a greater obligation to another party.

Resources and Needs

Section 3(6) of the Act expressly provides that, in considering the financial resources of any person, the court shall take into account his earning capacity, and in considering his financial needs, his financial obligations and responsibilities. There was authority under the 1938 Act for considering earning capacity, potential[7] as well as actual, but the second limb of the subsection is new. Can an applicant's obligations to his own family and dependants strengthen his claim as an applicant? Presumably they can, in an appropriate case. For example, a widowed daughter with young children would have a stronger claim to provision from her father's estate than a daughter who had no family or dependants.[8] On the other hand, where a woman and her child by the deceased are both applicants, an order in favour of the woman may make sufficient indirect provision for the child.[9]

The availability of State aid, for example under the National Health Service, is a factor to be taken into account in considering what provision is reasonable, by way of reducing the applicant's claim, because State aid is part of the resources of an applicant or beneficiary. However, it is only a factor, for extra comforts to be added to State provision may well be reasonable.[10]

Damages received for personal injuries are part of a person's resources.[11]

Expectations of capital in the future must, it is submitted, be considered by the court,[12] but often accretions of capital to the estate

---

[6] See, for example, *Banks* v. *Goodfellow* (1870) L.R. 5 Q.B. 549, 565. (A case on testamentary capacity.)

[7] *Re Ducksbury* [1966] 1 W.L.R. 1226.

[8] *Re Goard* (1962) 106 S.J. 721 may be another example, although the facts were rather special.

[9] *Bayliss* v. *Lloyds Bank* C.A., December 9, 1977, C.A.T. 77/978A.

[10] *Re E.* [1966] 1 W.L.R. 709; *Re Pringle, The Times*, February 2, 1956; *Re Parry, The Times*, April 19, 1956; *Re Wood* (1982) 79 L.S. Gaz. 774.

[11] *Daubney* v. *Daubney* [1976] Fam. 267.

[12] For an example under the matrimonial jurisdiction, see *Morgan* v. *Morgan* [1977] Fam. 122. It is submitted that the court has power to settle property on conditions or contingencies; for the power to settle property, see *post*, p. 49.

would best be dealt with after they have fallen in, on an application under section 6 of the Act for variation of the original order.[13] In order to preserve its power under section 6, the court must make an order for periodical payments on the original application, but a nominal order for a token amount would suffice for this purpose, if it is expressed in such a way that the accretion of capital is "relevant property" as defined in section 6(6).

Of all the needs of an applicant or beneficiary, the need for somewhere to live is likely to be especially important.[14]

The Obligations and Responsibilities of the Deceased

The fourth guideline is concerned with the moral duty of the deceased to applicants and beneficiaries, rather than with their own resources and needs. There may be more moral claims on the deceased than his estate can satisfy.[15] A common instance of conflict between these claims is that between the claims of wife and mistress, but there are other instances, such as that between the claims of spouse and children (usually children of a different marriage),[16] or even between parent and spouse.[17] The weight of one of the conflicting claims will be increased if a substantial part of the estate of the deceased was derived in some way from that claimant; for example, if a wife has helped the deceased to build up a business.[18] Similarly, the children of a first marriage have a stronger claim if a substantial part of the deceased's estate came to the deceased from their other parent,[19] and the children of the family have one if it came from their natural parent.[20]

Provision of capital in the past may reduce the strength of an applicant's claim.[21] On the other hand, the fact that an applicant (otherwise entitled to apply) was being maintained by the deceased may strengthen his claim. There was authority[22] under the 1938 Act that the use of the word "dependant" in that Act was significant, so that a factual relationship of dependency strengthened the claim of an applicant. There is no reason why the introduction by s. 1(1)(e) of the 1975 Act of a separate category of persons maintained should

---

[13] See *post*, p. 52.
[14] See *post*, pp. 37, 43, in connection with different categories of applicant.
[15] *Re Joslin* [1941] Ch. 200.
[16] *Re Singer* [1967] 1 W.L.R. 1482; *Re Bellman* [1963] P. 239.
[17] *Re Clarke* [1968] 1 W.L.R. 415.
[18] *Re Thornley* [1969] 1 W.L.R. 1037; for another example, see *Jelley* v. *Iliffe* [1981] Fam. 128.
[19] *Re Styler* [1942] Ch. 387; *Re Pugh* [1943] Ch. 387; *Re Sivyer* [1967] 1 W.L.R. 1482.
[20] *Re Leach* [1985] 3 W.L.R. 413; *Re Callaghan* [1985] Fam. 1.
[21] *Re E.* [1966] 1 W.L.R. 709; *Re Ducksbury* [1966] 1 W.L.R. 1226.
[22] *Re Gregory* [1970] 1 W.L.R. 1455.

affect this in relation to applicants in the other categories, and the existence of a factual relationship of dependency remains important.[23]

If the Court decides to make an order for the maintenance of an applicant, the amount of the maintenance received by him in the period before the death of the deceased is a very important factor in deciding what provision is reasonable after the death of the deceased. If the needs and means of an applicant remain as they were before the death of the deceased, and the net estate is sufficient for the purpose (taking into account the other claims on the deceased's bounty), it may well be reasonable that provision should continue at the same level[24] (although it may well be appropriate to capitalise the maintenance by making a lump sum order). However, the inadequate size of the net estate, or the strength of the other claims on the deceased's bounty, may invalidate this basis of measurement.[25] In any event, the basis cannot be elevated to a general rule of measurement, because the Act requires the Court to exercise its discretion by reference to the specified guidelines, rather than to any principle that levels of maintenance must be kept up.[26]

Size and Nature of the Estate

The reasonableness of any provision made or not made depends not only on the number and weight of the claims on the bounty of the deceased, but also upon the size of the estate available to satisfy them. A rich man can and in an appropriate case ought to make generous provision,[27] but a poor man may be justified in making no provision to satisfy a claim which would otherwise be strong. This is especially so if the major net effect of the provision would be a reduction in the applicant's social security benefits, leaving the applicant little better off.[28] If an estate is small there is still jurisdiction and the claim must be fully considered, but it will be material to consider (1) what state aid is available, (2) how far effective provision can be made, and (3) whether the costs are disproportionate.[29]

---

[23] *Re Fullard* [1982] Fam. 42.
[24] *Re Eyre* [1968] 1 W.L.R. 530, and the cases there cited; *Malone* v. *Harrison* [1979] 1 W.L.R. 1353.
[25] *Re E.*, *ante*, at p. 713, 714; *Re Borthwick* [1949] Ch. 395.
[26] *Re Crawford* (1983) 4 F.L.R. 273.
[27] *Re Borthwick* [1949] Ch. 395; *Re Black, The Times*, March 25, 1953; *Re Besterman* [1984] Ch. 458.
[28] *Re E.*, *ante*.
[29] *Re Clayton* [1966] 1 W.L.R. 969, 971.

Disability of an Applicant or Beneficiary

Disability may increase the need of a member of the deceased's family circle, and the obligation of the deceased towards him, so this guideline is implicit in guidelines (a) to (d). However, its inclusion as a separate guideline emphasises its importance,[30] and was also probably desirable because incapacity is not, as it was under the 1938 Act, a condition precedent to some applications.

Conduct and Other Matters

The concept of conduct is a vague and general one. Its relevance to the particular categories of spouses and children will be discussed later. At this point three aspects must be stressed. First, its very vagueness and generality. Secondly, the fact that this vagueness and generality does not create any difficulties for the Court. In appropriate cases the court takes conduct into account, and considers whether an applicant has been a good and loving wife,[31] or a dutiful child.[32] Thirdly, any reduction in the emphasis given to conduct may mean a step away from testamentary freedom, and towards the application of ideas of family property. For if conduct does not strengthen or weaken a claim for provision, then that claim must derive, to some extent at least, from the mere fact of relationship by blood, marriage, or dependency.

The 1938 Act required the court to have regard to the deceased's reasons for making the provision he did. The 1975 Act does not so require. It would fit ill with the objective nature of the test for reasonable provision. In so far as the deceased's reasons are good reasons, they will weigh with the court anyway. In so far as they are bad reasons, they will not, and may even rouse the court's hostility.[33] However, if a testator has good reasons for failing to make provision for a potential applicant, he can usefully make a written statement

---

[30] Note the somewhat surprising decision at first instance in *Millward* v. *Shenton* [1972] 1 W.L.R. 711, which perhaps suggests that an express mention of disability in the Act was desirable. It is suggested that an adult child's disability does give him a stronger claim; certainly this seems to be the approach of the courts. However, note the view of Tyler (ed. Oughton) at p. 179 that mere disability, even if causing financial hardship, ought not to be a ground for awarding provision to adult children.

[31] *Re Morris*, *The Times*, April 14, 1967; *Re Snoek* (1983) 13 Fam. Law 19.

[32] *Re Andrews* [1955] 1 W.L.R. 1105; *Re Cook* [1956] 106 L.J. 466. For a lengthy discussion of conduct as a factor under the 1938 Act, see Tyler, pp. 59–64.

[33] See, for example, *Re Borthwick* [1949] Ch. 395; *Re Clarke* [1968] 1 W.L.R. 415.

of them, to be kept with his will,[34] which will be admissible in evidence.[35]

Three "other matters" are worth specific mention. First, a promise or a non-contractual agreement by the deceased to dispose of his estate in a particular way will be taken into account by the Court, although it will not necessarily be decisive.[36] Secondly, the failure of a will to have the effect that the deceased expected may be material, and encourage the Court to make an order.[37] Thirdly, the Court will take account of any evidence of the deceased's expressions of intention to make provision for the applicant, especially when the fulfilment of that intention has been frustrated by supervening circumstances[38]; although again, this evidence will not necessarily be decisive.[39]

It is respectfully suggested that the Court is right to take account of evidence of the deceased's expressions of intention to make provision for an applicant, but ought to pay especial attention to its weight. To take an extreme example, it is one thing for the Court to intervene when the deceased has died the day before he was due to visit his solicitors to execute a will in favour of the applicant[40]; but another thing entirely for the Court to be influenced by vague expressions of intention which the deceased never took any steps to implement, although he could easily have done so.

As under the 1938 Act, testamentary capacity or the lack of it is not a matter which should be investigated on an application under the Act.[41] Feebleness of mind or understanding will not weigh with the court, because the test of reasonableness is objective.

Particular Guidelines: Surviving Spouse

Subsection 3(2) of the Act provides that, where an application is made by a spouse or former spouse, the court shall have regard to (a) the age of the applicant and the duration of the marriage; and

---

[34] Earlier wills are admissible and may be relevant. As to suppression of wills, see Williams, Mortimer and Sunnucks, p. 709.

[35] s. 21, and see p. 73, *post.*

[36] *Re Styler* [1942] Ch. 387; *Re Brown* [1955] 105 L.J. 169; and see *Jelley* v. *Iliffe* [1981] Fam. 128, 138, 140.

[37] *Re Goodwin* [1969] 1 Ch. 283; *Bayliss* v. *Lloyds Bank*, C.A. December 9, 1977. C.A.T. 77, 478A; and see *Re Besterman* [1984] Ch. 458, 465.

[38] *Re Callaghan* [1984] 3 W.L.R. 1076; *Re Coventry* [1980] Ch. 461, 490, commenting upon *Re Christie* [1979] Ch. 168.

[39] *Re Brindle* (1941) 192 L.T.J. 75.

[40] As in one case known to the author.

[41] *Re Blanch* [1967] 1 W.L.R. 987. If testamentary capacity is in issue, it can be decided in a Probate action heard immediately before the family provision hearing, and by the same Chancery judge: see p. 69, *post.*

(b) the contribution made by the applicant to the welfare of the family of the deceased, including any contribution made by looking after the home or caring for the family. Also, in the case of an application by a spouse, unless there was a continuing judicial separation, the subsection directs the court to have regard to the provision which the applicant might reasonably have expected to receive if on the date on which the deceased died, the marriage, instead of being terminated by death, had been terminated by a decree of divorce.[42]

The Particular Guidelines and the General Guidelines

The first two of these particular guidelines expressly direct the attention of the Court to matters which have already been put before it, by implication, in the general guidelines, and especially by that in section 3(1)(d). The age of the applicant, the duration of the marriage, and the contribution of the applicant's spouse to the welfare of the family of the deceased are all highly relevant to the obligations and responsibilities of the deceased to the applicant. Moreover, they are matters which influenced the Court under the 1938 and 1965 Acts.[43]

However the first two of the particular guidelines, and even more the third of them, are intended to do more than make express some matters which are implied by the general guidelines. They are a corollary to the wider definition of reasonable financial provision for spouses, as stated in section 1(2) of the Act. Together with that wider definition, they are intended to give a surviving spouse a claim upon the "family assets" at least equivalent to that of a divorced spouse.[44] The "family assets" are, as already explained,[45] those things which are acquired by one or other or both of the parties to the marriage, with the intention that they should be continuing provision for them and their children during their joint lives, and used for the benefit of the family as a whole.

Family Assets

The first two of the particular guidelines in effect repeat for the purposes of family provision law guidelines (d) and (f) in section

---

[42] For financial provision on divorce, see Miller, *Family Property and Financial Provision*; Jackson, *Matrimonial Finance and Taxation*; Cretney, *Principles of Family Law*.
[43] For examples, see *Bayliss* v. *Lloyds Bank* C.A., December 9, 1977, C.A.T. 77/478A; *Re Clarke* [1968] 1 W.L.R. 415; *Re Sylvester* [1941] Ch. 87; *Re Thornley* [1969] 1 W.L.R. 1037.
[44] Law Comm. 61, paras. 16, 27; (1984) 100 L.Q.R. 521.
[45] p. 00, *ante*.

25(1) of the Matrimonial Causes Act 1973,[46] namely "the age of each party to the marriage and duration of the marriage," and "the contributions made by each of the parties to the welfare of the family, including any contribution made by looking after the home or caring for the family." (Now re-enacted, with some modification, by the Matrimonial and Family Proceedings Act, 1984.) It must follow that the particular guidelines are apt to do what the corresponding guidelines do in the divorce jurisdiction, that is to enable the Court to award a spouse a share in the family assets by reason of that spouse's contribution to the welfare of the family in kind rather than in cash.[47] The spouse has earned her share, and the Court's powers enable it to award that share to her.

However, it is clear that the Divorce Court will not automatically make use of the concept of family assets. One Lord Justice has even gone so far as to observe that "family assets" is not now a phrase of any particular use.[48] It is respectfully suggested that the concept may still have some use, and influence the Court, in appropriate cases in both the divorce and the family provision jurisdictions[49], but that the primary task and obligation of the Court in both jurisdictions must be to have regard to the statutory guidelines.[50]

The concept of family assets is likely to influence the Court in applications under the 1975 Act if it would have influenced the Divorce Court, on the same facts, had the marriage been dissolved by divorce rather than by death. If on the same facts it would not have influenced the Divorce Court, then it is unlikely to influence the Court in family provision proceedings and, it is suggested, ought not to do so. Thus it will influence the Court in cases in which the parties to the marriage have started their married life with little or nothing but their earning capacities, and had together built up by their joint efforts such capital assets as they were able to acquire.[51] In this sort of case, one of the major assets will almost invariably be the matrimonial home, and the Court will be especially concerned (as under the divorce jurisdiction) to ensure that the applicant has a roof over his (or more usually her) head.

The concept of family assets will influence the Court much less in cases where one of the spouses has bought substantial capital assets

---

[46] Law Comm. 61, para. 32.

[47] See *Wachtel* v. *Wachtel* [1973] Fam. 72, 93, and generally.

[48] *P.* v. *P.* [1978] 1 W.L.R. 483, 487, per Ormrod L.J.

[49] See for example the remark of Purchas L.J. in *Stead* v. *Stead* [1985] F.L.R. 16, 23: "When one reviews the progress of the family wealth demonstrated from the evidence in this case...."

[50] As under the divorce jurisdiction: *O'D* v. *O'D* [1976] Fam. 83, 89; and see *P.* v. *P. ante*, 487 onwards.

[51] See *O'D* v. *O'D*, ante; and *Stead* v. *Stead*, ante, under the 1975 Act.

into the marriage, or has acquired such assets during the marriage by inheritance, gift or otherwise[52]; and in cases where the marriage has been short.[53] The concept is likely to be of little relevance in all these situations because the assets are not likely to be true "family assets"; they are not likely to have been acquired by the joint efforts of the parties for the joint benefit and use of themselves and their children. The concept will also have much less influence when "fossil marriages" are before the Court.[54] If cohabitation ended some time before the death of the deceased, and the parties to the marriage had arranged their lives on the footing that the marriage had ended, the family has come to an end as a unit for practical purposes, and the assets in the legal ownership of the parties cannot be described as "family assets." Similarly the concept is unlikely to be helpful where there has been, so to say, an accidental or inadvertent failure to make reasonable provision.[55] In such a situation, the deceased intended to make reasonable provision for his spouse, but delay in making the will, or supervening circumstances, have rendered unreasonable the provision made. The size of the estate, or the nature of the assets which make it up, may have had an unforeseen effect; or the circumstances of the surviving spouse or the other beneficiaries may have changed. The Court is more likely to seek to repair the consequences of the accident or inadvertence than to impose its own views as to the share of the family assets which ought to pass to the surviving spouse.

The One Third Starting Point

In considering the appropriate provision for a wife on divorce, the Court sometimes has a flexible starting point, or alternatively a guide with which to check a provisional conclusion. This is the starting point of one third of the capital assets of the parties, and

[52] Such as *O'D* v. *O'D, ante*; for other examples under the divorce jurisdiction, see *Trippas* v. *Trippas* [1973] Fam. 134 and *Calderbank* v. *Calderbank* [1976] Fam. 93; for examples under the family provision jurisdiction, see *Re Bunning* [1984] Ch. 480 and *Re Besterman* [1984] Ch. 458.
[53] As in the divorce case of *S.* v. *S.* [1977] Fam. 127. But some capital provision may be proper: see *S.* v. *S.* itself; *Cumbers* v. *Cumbers* [1974] 1 W.L.R. 1331; and *Re Chatterton*, C.A., November 1, 1978, C.A.T. 78/660 (a case under the 1975 Act).
[54] As in the divorce case of *Krystman* v. *Krystman* [1973] 1 W.L.R. 927. For examples of such marriages see *Re Gregory* [1970] 1 W.L.R. 1455 (under the 1938 Act) and *Re Rowlands* [1984] F.L.R. 813 (under the 1975 Act).
[55] For examples see *Re Goodwin* [1969] 1 Ch. 283; *Re Lewis*, C.A., March 13, 1980, C.A.T. 80/158 (where inflation was the supervening circumstance). See also pp. 23, 32, *ante*.

one third of the joint earnings. It is related to the concept of family assets. As Lord Denning M.R. said in *Wachtel* v. *Wachtel*[56]:

> "If we were only concerned with the capital assets of the family, and particularly with the matrimonial home, it would be tempting to divide them half and half. . . . That would be fair enough if the wife afterwards went her own way, making no further demands on the husband. It would be simply a division of the assets of the partnership. That may come in the future. But at present few wives are content with a share of the capital assets. Most wives want their former husbands to make periodical payments as well to support them; because, after the divorce, he will be earning far more than she; and she can only keep up her standard of living with his help. He also has to make payments for the children out of his earnings, even if they are with her. In view of those calls on his future earnings, we do not think she can have both—half the capital assets, and half the earnings . . . Giving it the best consideration we can, we think that the fairest way is to start with one third of each. If she has one third of the family assets of her own—and one third of the joint earnings—her past contributions are adequately recognised, and her future living standards assured so far as may be. She will certainly in this way be as well off as if the capital assets were divided equally—which is all that a partner is entitled to."

Under the family provision jurisdiction the Court cannot make use of the same starting point, because the deceased has no more earnings. However, it can and does pay some regard to the reasoning behind it, and in particular to the idea that one third of the capital assets of the family and one third of the joint earnings are a substitute for half the capital assets. On death, if the concept of family assets is relevant to the marriage in question, an order which puts a half of the joint capital assets at the disposal of the surviving spouse, either absolutely or for life, may well make reasonable financial provision. At least, this may well be a useful guide or cross check.[57]

The Relevance of the Need for Maintenance

As has already been observed, the three particular guidelines are

---

[56] [1973] Fam. 72, 95.
[57] *Re Bunning* [1984] Ch. 480, 499; *Re Besterman* [1984] Ch. 458, 473; *Stead* v. *Stead* [1985] F.L.R. 16, 27.

intended to give a surviving spouse a claim upon the family assets at least equivalent to that of a divorced spouse.[58] So is the wider definition of reasonable financial provision for spouses in section 1(2) of the Act. However, this does not mean that reasonable financial provision for a spouse is provision for maintenance only, should the spouse not have made a significant contribution to the family assets. Even if she has not earned her share, she is entitled to reasonable financial provision measured by the more generous standard. This follows from the terms of the Act, whereby the wider definition of reasonable financial provision applies to all spouses. Moreover, the reported cases[59] show that the court makes awards in accordance with the more generous standard, even though the spouse has not made a significant direct or indirect contribution to the deceased's assets, nor any especial contribution to the welfare of the family.[60]

Although reasonable financial provision for a spouse must be measured by a more generous standard than the need for maintenance, that need is likely to loom the larger before the Court, the smaller the estate. As Purchas L.J. observed in *Stead* v. *Stead*,[61] "where the estate is of more modest proportions, the margin available from which the Court is able to make provision in excess of that required for reasonable maintenance of the surviving spouse as indicated by section 1(2)(*a*) of the Act is considerably reduced." At the other end of the scale, where resources are very large, the awards required for reasonable financial provision probably begin to "level off," as in the divorce jurisdiction.[62] Reasonable financial provision for the widow of a millionaire may well be much less than one third of the capital available for distribution, unless perhaps her contribution to the family assets has been very great.

Whether the estate of the deceased is large or small, the Court is likely to be especially concerned to ensure that the applicant spouse has satisfactory accommodation.[63] Also, if it makes a lump sum order, it will seek to ensure, so far as possible, that the lump sum is sufficient to make allowance for future contingencies, and for inflation.[64] When the spouse is elderly and the beneficiaries are the

---

[58] See p. 33, *ante.*
[59] *Re Besterman, ante,* is the strongest authority; see also to some extent *Re Bunning, ante.*
[60] For interesting criticisms of the decision of the Court of Appeal in *Re Besterman* in relation to this, see Tyler (ed. Oughton) at p. 312 onwards.
[61] [1985] F.L.R. 16, 22.
[62] *Re Besterman, ante,* citing *Preston* v. *Preston* [1982] Fam. 17, 28.
[63] See generally *Re Besterman, ante,* and *Re Bunning, ante.*
[64] *Re Besterman, ante,* 298.

adult children of the deceased, it is suggested that most or all of the provision may best be made by way of a life interest.[65]

The Relevance of Conduct

Under the original section 25 of the Matrimonial Causes Act 1973, there was strong authority that the conduct of the parties was irrelevant to financial provision, unless it was obvious and gross.[66] Under the new section 25, enacted by section 3 of the Matrimonial and Family Proceedings Act 1984, the Divorce Court is directed to have regard to "the conduct of each of the parties, if that conduct is such that it would in the opinion of the Court be inequitable to disregard it." The effect of this change in the law is uncertain, as far as the divorce jurisdiction is concerned; probably it will not be very great in practice.

Under the influence of the divorce jurisdiction, questions of conduct appear to have become less important in applications by spouses under the 1975 Act.[67] However, conduct which is obvious and gross, or such that it would in the opinion of the Court be inequitable to disregard it, will certainly influence the Court.[68] Moreover, conduct may well have to play a somewhat larger part in the family provision jurisdiction than in the divorce jurisdiction, for two reasons. First, general guideline (d) directs the Court to consider the obligations and responsibilities of the deceased to applicants and beneficiaries. These obligations and responsibilities must be affected by the conduct of applicants and beneficiaries. Secondly, the concept of conduct in the divorce jurisdiction is a concept with a core of more or less clear and restricted meaning: that core is the conduct which provided grounds for divorce before the Divorce Reform Act 1969.[69] Indeed, the great reduction in the importance of conduct in the divorce jurisdiction derived from the change made in the grounds for divorce in that Act.[70] But outside the context of divorce proceedings, the concept of conduct loses this core of meaning. It becomes vague and general; a person's conduct is everything about the way he behaves.

A Former Spouse

The first and second, but not the third, of the particular guidelines

[65] *S.* v. *S., ante; Stead* v. *Stead, ante;* see also p. 29, *ante.*
[66] *Wachtel* v. *Wachtel, ante,* at 89.
[67] See for example *Re Bunning, ante; Stead* v. *Stead, ante.*
[68] *Re Snoek* (1983) 13 Fam. Law 19.
[69] However, conduct is not restricted to this meaning: *Jones (M.A.)* v. *Jones (W.)* [1976] Fam. 8.
[70] *Wachtel* v. *Wachtel, ante,* 89.

for applications by spouses are also specified for former spouses. The court is to have regard to (a) the age of the former spouse and the duration of the marriage and (b) the contribution made by the former spouse to the welfare of the family of the deceased, including any contribution made by looking after the home or caring for the family.[71] Since the general standard of provision for former spouses is the maintenance standard, these guidelines are not apt to support a claim by a former spouse to a share in the family assets.

In *Re Fullard*[72] the Court of Appeal observed that the Divorce Court now has power to make appropriate adjustments as between spouses after divorce, and that therefore the number of cases in which it is possible for a former spouse to apply successfully under the 1975 Act is comparatively small. The Court of Appeal gave as examples of applications which might succeed ones in which periodical payments have been made for a long time,[73] and there is a reasonable amount of capital in the estate; and ones in which substantial capital funds are unlocked by the death of the deceased, because of insurance or pension policies.

It is difficult to think of other circumstances in which a former spouse could apply successfully. The mere fact of accretion of wealth after the dissolution of the marriage is unlikely to be sufficient of itself to justify an application.[74] Possibly concealment by the deceased of his true financial position would have some significance[75]. Just possibly the applicant's mere ignorance of an improvement in the deceased's financial circumstances would weigh with the Court; or a great disparity between the resources and needs of the former spouse and the beneficiaries; or help and support by the former spouse after the divorce.[76] However, it is suggested that only a combination of more than one of these other circumstances is at all likely to give rise to a situation in which a former spouse could apply successfully.

In *Re Eyre*[77] the Court observed that (1) an order for secured maintenance, made on divorce, ought not to be treated as a

---

[71] s. 3(2).
[72] [1982] Fam. 42; [1982] Conv. 75.
[73] Of course an application may not succeed, even though periodical payments have ended with the death of the deceased: *Re Talbot* [1962] 1 W.L.R. 113.
[74] *Re Fullard* at 52. For cases of accretion of wealth under the 1938 and 1965 Acts, see *Re Borthwick* [1949] Ch. 395; *Re Whittle*, C.A., March 5, 1973, C.A.T. 73/94A; *Re Eyre* [1968] 1 W.L.R. 530.
[75] In *Brill* v. *Proud* [1984] 14 Fam. Law such concealment was alleged, but the allegation was not made out. The secretiveness of the deceased about his financial affairs appears to have had some weight with the Court in *Re W* [1975] 119 Sol. Jo. 436, an application by a former spouse under the 1965 Act.
[76] *Re Bellman* [1963] P. 239.
[77] [1968] 1 W.L.R. 530.

predetermination of what a survivor should receive after the death of a former spouse; (2) there could not be any general rule that a first wife should be accorded financial equality with a widow; (3) contrariwise, a lack of parity between the financial position of a first and a second wife during the lifetime of the husband should not of itself be treated as sufficient reason for prolonging that position after his death; and (4) assuming that the former wife's needs and her means remain as they were before the husband's death, and assuming that the net estate is sufficient for the purpose, then it is reasonable that she should continue to receive the same provision as during the husband's lifetime, sufficiency being determined having regard to the provision for or needs of other claimants on the husband's bounty. It is submitted that the reported cases on the 1975 Act, especially *Re Fullard* [78] and *Re Crawford*,[79] have left the force of the first observation untouched, and have strengthened that of the second, but have weakened that of the third and fourth.[80]

A Child or Person Treated as a Child

These two categories can be considered together. The guideline common to them both is that the court is directed to have regard to the manner in which the applicant was being or in which he might expect to be educated or trained.[81] Presumably some applicants might expect to receive private education,[82] others not, and in relation to this the other claims on the deceased, and the size of the estate, are obviously relevant. In relation to higher education, for which grants from central or local government might be available to an applicant, presumably the court's approach will be similar to that already adopted towards the government provision of social security benefits[83]: the student may be awarded money for extra comforts, but not so as merely to reduce his grant.

Under the 1938 Act, the conduct of a child could be relevant as increasing his or her claim, for instance if a daughter had made sacrifices to look after the deceased.[84] It could also reduce the claim, for example, if contact had not been close or the child had not

---

[78] [1982] Fam. 42.
[79] [1983] 4 F.L.R. 273.
[80] See also p. 30, *ante.*
[81] s. 3(3).
[82] See *Bosch* v. *Perpetual Trustee Co. Ltd.* [1938] A.C. 463; compare private medical care: *Re Sanderson* [1963] C.L.Y. 3624.
[83] See p. 28, *ante.*
[84] *Re Cook* (1956) 106 L.J. 466.

been dependent on the deceased for some time.[85] It is submitted that conduct ought to and will continue to be relevant in these respects.[86]

The Act specifies three further guidelines for applications by persons who were not children of the deceased, but were treated as such.[87] The court is to have regard (a) to whether the deceased had assumed any responsibility for the applicant's maintenance and, if so, the extent to which and the basis upon which the deceased assumed that responsibility and to the length of time for which he discharged that responsibility; (b) to whether in assuming and discharging that responsibility the deceased did so knowing that the applicant was not his own child; and (c) to the liability of any other person to maintain the applicant. These guidelines correspond with those laid down for the matrimonial jurisdiction by the Matrimonial Causes Act 1973.[88]

The introduction of the new category of persons treated as children raises the question whether their claims will be weaker than those of true children; in other words, whether the blood tie is of itself significant. It is submitted that, since the blood tie is not mentioned in the Act, it ought to have less weight than the guidelines which do appear there.[89] The claims of true children may well be stronger in most cases anyway, by reason of the operation of the specified guidelines, both general and particular.

Re Coventry[90] is authority for the proposition that, where a child or person treated as a child is an adult male in employment, and so capable of earning his own living, some special circumstance is required to render unreasonable a failure on the part of the deceased to make some financial provision for the child. The same applies, it is submitted, where the child is an adult female capable of earning her own living. But perhaps there might be an argument in favour of some small provision for such a child at the outset of his or her independent life.[91]

Under the 1938 Act, the Court sometimes considered that the claim on the bounty of the deceased of a child who was a beneficiary under his will was relatively stronger in relation to the claim of an applicant who was a surviving spouse (and a stepparent) if a substantial part of the estate of the deceased was derived

[85] *Re Andrews* [1955] 1 W.L.R. 1105; *Re Ducksbury* [1966] 1 W.L.R. 1226.
[86] This view is shared by J. G. Miller: see *Current Law Statutes* (1975), notes to s. 3.
[87] s. 3(3).
[88] s. 25(4) of that Act, as amended.
[89] But it did apparently have some weight under the 1938 and 1965 Acts: *Re Harker-Thomas* [1969] P. 28, 31.
[90] [1980] Ch. 461.
[91] See *ante*, p. 20.

from the child's other parent.[92] In one reported case,[93] the Court was influenced in the same way in the converse situation, when the child was the applicant, and the step-parent the beneficiary. The child was only 15 years old, so the case is consistent with *Re Coventry*. However, in two recent cases under the 1975 Act, *Re Leach*[94] and *Re Callaghan*,[95] adults who were not in any special need applied for provision out of the estate of their step-parent, they being qualified to do so as persons treated as children of the family by the step-parent. In both cases the step-parent died intestate and collateral members of the step-parent's family were the beneficiaries. In each case, the Court made a substantial order in favour of the applicant, being strongly influenced by the fact that the deceased's estate was partly derived from the applicant's natural parent. The decisions are very understandable, because it is hard that property should pass right out of a family through the intervention of a step-parent. However, they are not easy to reconcile with *Re Coventry*.[96]

A Person Maintained by the Deceased

This new category is potentially a very wide one. However, as has already been mentioned,[97] its operation is restricted by its one particular guideline, whereby the court is directed to have regard to the extent to which, and the basis upon which, the deceased assumed responsibility for the maintenance of the applicant, and to the length of time for which the deceased discharged that responsibility.[98] In *Re Beaumont*,[99] Megarry V.-C. held that an applicant was not entitled to apply at all unless the deceased had assumed responsibility for his or her maintenance, and that the burden of establishing such an assumption of responsibility lay upon the applicant. However in *Jelley* v. *Iliffe*[1] the Court of Appeal

[92] *Re Styler* [1942] Ch. 387; *Re Pugh* [1943] Ch. 387.
[93] *Re Sivyer* [1967] 1 W.L.R. 1482.
[94] [1985] 3 W.L.R. 413.
[95] [1985] Fam. 1.
[96] The actual decision in *Re Callaghan* can be strongly defended on the ground that the deceased clearly intended to make a will in favour of the applicant, and was in effect prevented from doing so by illness, in circumstances which were very creditable to the applicant. However, the learned judge did not put this in the forefront of her reasoning.
[97] See p. 23, ante.
[98] s. 3(4).
[99] [1980] Ch. 444; (1980) 96 L.Q.R. 534 (a whole review article on this and other cases under s. 1(1)(e)); (1982) 12 Fam. Law 158 (discussing contributions and considerations.).
[1] [1981] Fam. 128.

took a different approach, holding that the mere maintenance of the applicant by the deceased usually means that the deceased has assumed that responsibility. The Court of Appeal does not appear to have considered the question whether an express disclaimer of responsibility would automatically disqualify an applicant, or merely be a factor for the court to consider in the exercise of its discretion.

As well as showing an assumption of responsibility, an applicant in this category of course has to prove that the deceased was making a substantial contribution in money or money's worth towards his or her reasonable needs, and was doing so otherwise than for full valuable consideration. This does not merely go to the reasonableness of the provision made or not made by the deceased, and to the discretion of the court, but to the prior question of the applicant's right to apply at all.

If the estate is sufficient, it appears that the award made to a successful applicant in this category will reflect the degree of the applicant's dependence on the deceased before his death.[2]

However, the Court is also concerned, as with applicants in other categories, to ensure that the person maintained has somewhere to live.[3] In addition, the Court may be influenced by similarities between the relationship of the deceased and the applicant and the more formal relationships of marriage and parenthood.[4] It may also be influenced by the help and comfort the applicant gave to the deceased, and their future plans together.[5]

The facts of such cases as *Re Beaumont, supra*, and *Jelley* v. *Iliffe, supra*, suggest that the guidelines in section 3 of the Act give little if any indication of the weight which should be given to the claims of a person maintained by the deceased as against the claims of beneficiaries who are close relatives of the deceased but in no great financial need, as might be, perhaps, adult children of the deceased. It is submitted that beneficiaries who are children of the deceased have a moral claim to their parents' estates, even if not themselves in need, and that the court ought to recognise their claims. Parliament surely cannot have intended that the claims of "an elderly housekeeper . . . a nephew . . . a widowed sister . . ."[6] should necessarily prevail over those of the children of the deceased, being beneficiaries under his will or intestacy, just because the children were in no great financial need.

[2] *Malone* v. *Harrison* [1979] 1 W.L.R. 1353 (1980) L.Q.R. 165.
[3] *Re Haig* (1979) 129 New L.J. 420; *Harrington* v. *Gill* (1983) 4 F.L.R. 265.
[4] *Re McC, CA* v. *CC* "*The Times*", November 17, 1978; (1979) 9 Fam. Law 26; (1979) 123 Sol. Jo. 35.
[5] *Williams* v. *Roberts* (1984) Fam. Law 210.
[6] See pp. 22, 23, ante.

Certainly in one case the Court has balanced the claims of an applicant against those of the daughter of the deceased, the sole beneficiary, by awarding the greater part of the provision in the form of life interests.[7]

[7] *Harrington* v. *Gill, ante.*

5 Orders Which the Court can Make

Under the 1975 Act the court can make any one or more of the following orders[1]:

(a) an order for the making to the applicant out of the net estate of the deceased of such periodical payments and for such term as may be specified in the order;

(b) an order for the payment to the applicant out of that estate of a lump sum of such amount as may be so specified;

(c) an order for the transfer to the applicant of such property comprised in that estate as may be so specified;

(d) an order for the settlement for the benefit of the applicant of such property comprised in that estate as may be so specified;

(e) an order for the acquisition out of property comprised in that estate of such property as may be so specified and for the transfer of the property so acquired to the applicant or for the settlement thereof for his benefit;

(f) an order varying any ante-nuptial or post-nuptial settlement (including such a settlement made by will) made on the parties to a marriage to which the deceased was one of the parties, the variation being for the benefit of the surviving party to that marriage, or any child of that marriage, or any person who was treated by the deceased as a child of the family in relation to that marriage.

Under the 1938 Act and the 1965 Act the court could only make one or both of the first two orders, an order for periodical payments or a lump sum payment. The new wider powers of the court correspond with the powers to make orders given to the court in the matrimonial jurisdiction by the Matrimonial Causes Act 1973,[2] and the reported cases on the exercise of the powers in that jurisdiction should be of assistance in the family provision jurisdiction.

[1] s. 6(2).
[2] ss. 23(1), 24(1) of that Act.

Periodical Payments

An order for periodical payments may provide for[3] (a) payment of such amount as may be specified in the order (*e.g.* £100 a month),[4] or (b) payments equal to the whole of the income of the net estate or of such portion thereof as may be so specified (*e.g.* one-third of the income of the net estate) or (c) payments equal to the whole of the income of such part of the net estate as the court may direct to be set aside or appropriated for the making, out of the income thereof, of periodical payments (*e.g.* the whole of the income of one-third of the net estate, such one-third of the net estate being appropriated). Alternatively, the order may provide for the amount of the payments or any of them to be determined in any other way the court thinks fit. It is a little difficult to envisage a way other than the three stated, but perhaps one example would be an order which provided for fluctuating payments not directly proportionate to the income of the estate; for example, one-third if the income is below a certain sum, but one-half if it rises above that sum. The retail price index could even be used in some way; but such sophisticated orders are likely to be rare.

It is expressly provided[4a] that the order for periodical payments may direct that a specified part of the net estate shall be set aside or appropriated for the making, out of the income thereof, of the periodical payments.[5] However, no larger part of the net estate is to be set aside or appropriated than is sufficient, at the date of the order, to produce by the income thereof the amount required for the making of the payments. This provision is the nearest to the provision in the Matrimonial Causes Act 1973[6] which gives the court power to secure periodical payments. Such a power to secure is less necessary in the family provision jurisdiction because the estate of the deceased is held by personal representatives who are in a position of trusteeship.

The periodical payments are to be for a term specified in the order. Normally, no doubt, the term will begin with the death of the deceased, but this is not essential; provision could, for instance, be ordered from the date of the judgment,[7] or from the end of the

---

[3] s. 2(2).
[4] In an appropriate case, an order may be made for periodical payments in excess of the income of the estate: *Re F* (1965) 109 S.J. 212.
[4a] s. 2(3).
[5] If real property is to be appropriated, care must be taken to get the conveyancing right. For example, the appropriation may require a trust for sale or a strict settlement to be set up.
[6] s. 23(1)(*b*) of that Act.
[7] *Re Lecoche* (1967) 111 S.T. 136; *Lusternik* v. *Lusternik* [1972] Fam. 125. But see p. 77, *post*; difficulties may arise on administration if the date of judgment is chosen.

"executor's year" of 12 months after the death. As for the end of the term, the Act itself provides that an order in favour of a former spouse shall, in so far as it provides for the making of periodical payments, cease to have effect on the remarriage of that former spouse, except in relation to any arrears.[8] The same applies in cases of judicial separation. But apart from this, no time is fixed by the Act for the ending of the term. The court must decide it when it makes the order. Therefore, for example, an order for periodical payments in favour of a surviving spouse does not automatically terminate on remarriage, although the court could in its order have made the term end on future remarriage. Likewise orders in favour of children or persons treated as children of the family will not automatically terminate on the attainment of full age or marriage, although again the court could have made any particular order so terminate. The end of the term for the periodical payments is thus, with the one exception for former spouses and judicially separated spouses, left to be fixed when the order is made. However, it is difficult if not impossible to think of a case in which it would be right for the court to order that the term should continue after the death of the applicant.

Orders for periodical payments may be subsequently varied under the power given by section 6 of the Act; this power is explained, *post*.[9] The power to vary extends to a variation of the date or event originally fixed by the court for the end of the term of the periodical payments, because the fixing of that date or event is part of the order of the court.[10] However, the power to vary does not allow the court to vary or give a dispensation from the rule that orders in favour of former spouses and judicially separated spouses terminate on remarriage, because that rule is part of the Act itself.[11]

Lump Sums

The power to award provision for maintenance by way of an order for payment of a lump sum existed under the 1938 Act and the 1965 Act. In some decided cases under the 1938 Act the court stressed that lump sums were to be awarded by way of maintenance,[12] and this approach ought logically to be followed in cases under the new Act where the applicants are only entitled to claim the maintenance

---

[8] s. 19(2). This may be an important consideration in litigation and negotiation.
[9] pp. 52, 53, *post*.
[10] s. 6(3).
[11] s. 6(3).
[12] *Re Sivyer* [1967] 1 W.L.R. 1482, 1487.

standard of provision (that is, of course, all applicants other than
surviving spouses).[13] Under the 1938 Act there was a tendency to
consider lump sums more appropriate in applications relating to
small estates.[14] This tendency may have derived from the original
restriction of lump sum orders to cases in which the net estate did
not exceed £2,000. It is submitted that the tendency will exist in so
far as a small estate can most effectively make provision by means
of a lump sum payment, but ought not to, and will not, prevent the
award of a lump sum from a medium sized or large estate, in so far
as such an award would be otherwise appropriate. This is especially
so in applications by surviving spouses.[15] In such applications, the
practice of the court in ordering lump sums under the Matrimonial
Causes Act 1973 may provide useful guidance,[16] provided as always
that caution is exercised in comparing the two jurisdictions.

It appears to be permissible, and could sometimes be appropriate, to order payment of a lump sum equivalent to the whole of
the net estate; for example, where the deceased died intestate,
leaving a small estate, the claimant is a mistress who has lived with
him as his wife for many years, and the beneficiaries are distant
relatives who never knew him. In *Millward* v. *Shenton*[17] the Court of
Appeal ordered a lump sum equivalent to eleven-twelfths of the net
estate, the beneficiary being a charity, and the applicant a disabled
son.

A lump sum order can provide for the payment of the lump sum
by instalments.[18] The number, amounts, and dates for payment of
the instalments can be varied on a subsequent application for
variation; apart from this, a lump sum order cannot be varied.

Where a lump sum was awarded in lieu of maintenance under the
1938 Act, the practice was to begin with the figure and term
appropriate for annual maintenance and deduce from this the value
of such an interest. This appears to be the only logical approach to
the assessment of the appropriate sum when the applicant is only
entitled to the maintenance standard of provision.[19] *Malone* v.
Harrison[20] suggests that it will be the practice under the new Act.

[13] See *Re Besterman* [1984] Ch. 458, 465.
[14] *Re Sivyer, ante; Re Clayton* [1966] 1 W.L.R. 969.
[15] Not least because of the concept of family assets: see pp. 33–35, *ante.*
[16] See pp. 33–38, *ante,* and Miller, *Family Property and Financial Provision*; Jackson, *Matrimonial Finance and Taxation* and Cretney, *Principles of Family Law.*
[17] [1972] 1 W.L.R. 711.
[18] s. 7. A lump sum may also be charged on property and the enforcement of the charge deferred: *Re H.* (1975) 120 S.J. 81.
[19] An annuity table could be used, or the advice of an actuary sought.
[20] [1979] 1 W.L.R. 1353.

Transfer of Property

An order for the transfer of a specific item of property is especially useful when a lump sum order would necessitate an improvident realisation of part of the estate. "Property" has a wide meaning. It includes a chose in action[21]; thus, presumably, an order under the Act could in effect forgive a debt owed to the deceased by a person entitled to apply for provision, by directing the debt to be transferred to him. Under the Matrimonial Causes Act 1973, "property" also includes a weekly contractual tenancy, whether granted by a private landlord or a local authority,[22] and it is submitted that the position must be the same under the family provision jurisdiction.

An order for the transfer of property cannot be varied, but such an order can be made, although not made originally, on an application to vary a previous order for periodical payments.[23]

The court can make an order which is in effect the grant of an option. In *Re Kozdrach, Sobesto* v. *Farren*[24] the applicant had been living with the deceased as his wife. His dwelling-house was worth £28,000 at the date of the hearing. The court awarded the applicant a lump sum of £18,000, and ordered that she could within 6 months apply for a transfer of the dwelling-house at a price of £9,000.

Settlement of Property

An order for the settlement of property is especially appropriate when an applicant is a minor, or needs to be protected for some other reason. However, it can be useful in other situations. Care must be taken by those advising applicants and beneficiaries to see that the settlement is well drafted from the point of view of trust and tax law; it would be a pity if, for example, a settlement on a child applicant failed to take full advantage of the capital transfer tax advantages provided by an accumulation and maintenance trust

---

[21] s. 25(1).

[22] *Hale* v. *Hale* [1975] 1 W.L.R. 931 (private landlord); *Thompson* v. *Thompson* [1976] Fam. 25 (local authority landlord). However, in cases where the landlord can and does refuse his consent to an assignment, the court ought not to make an order for the transfer of the tenancy. Also, the court should not make orders in respect of council tenancies which put pressure on councils or which may be rejected by councils: *Regan* v. *Regan* [1977] 1 W.L.R. 84. But *quaere* whether this case would be followed now that council tenants and their families have security of tenure and rights of succession under the Housing Act 1980.

[23] s. 6(2).

[24] [1981] Conv. 224.

which satisfies the requirements of section 71 of the Capital Transfer Tax Act 1984.[25]

The power to order a settlement of property, together with the other powers given to the court, will authorise the creation of a charge on the property, as is the case under the matrimonial jurisdiction.[26]

An order for the settlement of property cannot be varied, nor can such an order be made on an application to vary an existing order for periodical payments.

Acquisition of Property

An order for the acquisition of property, and its transfer to or settlement upon an applicant, will be useful when the applicant needs a home, for example, when a surviving spouse wants to move to a smaller house.[27]

The order cannot be varied,[28] nor can such an order be made on an application to vary an order for periodical payments.

Variation of Settlements

The meaning of the phrase "ante-nuptial or post-nuptial settlement" has been made tolerably clear by a series of cases under the matrimonial jurisdiction. However, it is difficult to give a short and simple explanation of the phrase, because it extends beyond settlements as understood by conveyancers, although it includes them. Briefly, it means some document or transaction (other than an absolute gift) providing for the financial benefit of one or other or both of the spouses concerned as spouses and with reference to their married state, prospective or actual. The settlement must be made in contemplation of or because of marriage and with reference to the interests of married people or their children.[29]

The court's power to vary the settlement is restricted, because the variation must be for the benefit of the surviving party to the

---

[25] Formerly Finance Act 1975, Sched. 6, para. 15. For Capital Transfer Tax, see generally Wheatcroft and Hewson, *Encyclopedia of Capital Taxation;* Dymond, *Capital Transfer Tax.*

[26] *Hector* v. *Hector* [1973] 1 W.L.R. 1122, and see *Re H* n. 18, p. 48, *ante.*

[27] Law Comm. 61, para. 116.

[28] But if the trusts constitute a settlement under the Settled Land Act 1925 the life tenant will have the powers of a tenant for life under that Act (including the power of sale) unless the order deprives him of them. See *Re Hills* [1941] W.N. 123; *Re Mason* (1975) 5 Fam. Law 124.

[29] See generally Miller, *Family Property and Financial Provision,* and the cases there cited, especially *Prinsep* v. *Prinsep* [1929] P. 225, 232, and *Hargreaves* v. *Hargreaves* [1926] P. 42, 45; Cretney, *Principles of Family Law,* p. 753.

marriage concerned, or any child of that marriage, or any person who is treated by the deceased as a child of the family in relation to that marriage.[30] Thus an applicant only entitled to apply as a dependant of the deceased cannot seek a variation of such a settlement in his or her quest for reasonable provision.

An order for the variation of an ante-nuptial or post-nuptial settlement cannot itself be varied, nor can it be made on an application to vary a previous order for periodical payments.[31]

Burden of Orders

If the court is to make an order for provision which balances the claims of applicants against those of the existing beneficiaries under the will or intestacy, and treat the members of both classes as fairly as possible, it must have power to apportion the burden of its order among the existing beneficiaries in the way it thinks right. Such an apportionment was possible under the 1938 Act and the 1965 Act, and was practised by the court.[32] Such beneficiaries will of course have to be joined as parties and this can often raise problems as to whether in particular mere pecuniary legatees should be made defendants.[33] Apportionment now receives statutory authority. The order may contain such consequential and supplemental provisions as the court thinks necessary or expedient for giving effect to the order or securing that the order operates fairly as between one beneficiary of the estate and another, and may, in particular, (a) order any person who holds any property which forms part of the net estate of the deceased to make such payment or transfer such property as may be specified in the order[34]; (b) vary the disposition of the deceased's estate effected by the will or the intestacy rules, or both will and intestacy rules, as the court thinks fair and reasonable having regard to the provisions of the order and all the circumstances of the case; and (c) confer on the trustees of any property which is the subject of an order such powers as appear to the court to be necessary or expedient.[35]

---

[30] s. 2(1)(f).
[31] As a matter of general law a settlement can of course be varied by agreement if all parties are of full capacity, and if not, then maybe under the Variation of Trusts Act 1958.
[32] Re Westby [1946] W.N. 141; and see post p. 73.
[33] Re Preston [1969] 1 W.L.R. 317. In Re Lidington [1940] Ch. 927, an order was made in favour of a surviving spouse on terms that she maintained her children by the deceased, who were beneficiaries under his will.
[34] It is submitted that the court could order a specific legatee of the shares in a company to make a money payment to the applicant.
[35] s. 2(4). See also n. 18, p. 48, ante.

Variation of Orders

Section 6 of the Act gives a limited power to vary existing orders.[36] The essence of the power is that, if an order for periodical payments has been made, the court can on a subsequent application either make a new order for periodical payments payable out of the property out of which the existing periodical payments are payable; or order a lump sum payment out of that property[37]; or order a transfer of the property, or part of it. Thus the property out of which provision has to be made—called in the section "relevant property"—cannot be increased.[38] To some extent this preserves the advantages of finality, in the sense that the variation of an order already made cannot take more property out of the estate, which would make administration impossible. By contrast, the right to apply is not restricted to existing successful applicants. It extends to (a) any person originally entitled to apply; (b) the personal representatives of the deceased; (c) the trustees of any "relevant property"; and (d) any beneficiary of the estate.[39] Moreover, the power to vary can be exercised repeatedly.[40] The power to vary can only affect property which is applicable for the making of periodical payments. Thus it cannot affect a dwelling-house in which the applicant is allowed to live under the terms of the original order.[41]

The right to apply for a variation lasts for six months after the periodical payments have terminated under the original order, but there is no power to vary an order for periodical payments so as to extend them beyond the remarriage of a former spouse (as distinct from the remarriage of a surviving spouse).[42]

The power to vary could have strange results if one application against an estate is made within the six-month time limit imposed by section 4 of the Act, and another application is made by a different applicant outside the time limit. If the second applicant is not given an extension of time, he cannot apply while the first application is pending. But if and when an order for periodical payments is made at the hearing of the first application, the second applicant can then apply for its variation. Perhaps the practical answer to the problem is that, when one application is already

---

[36] Including orders (other than interim orders) made under the 1938 and 1965 Acts: see s. 26(4).

[37] Presumably, even if a lump sum order, as well as the periodical payments order, had been made on the original application.

[38] s. 6(6).

[39] s. 6(5). Conditions as to notifying the trustees of changes in circumstances may be included in the order: *Re Hills* [1941] W.N. 123.

[40] s. 6(4).

[41] *Re Fricker* (1982) 3 F.L.R. 228.

[42] s. 6(3).

pending, further applicants will be given extensions of time if their applications have any chance of success.

When the court varies an order for periodical payments, it must have regard to all the circumstances of the case, including any change in circumstances which would alter the effect of the general guidelines or any relevant particular guidelines.[43]

As already mentioned, orders for the settlement of property, the acquisition of property, or the variation of an ante-nuptial or post-nuptial settlement cannot be made on an application to vary an order for periodical payments.[44] Nor can orders be made affecting property held on joint tenancy, nor can orders be made under the powers[45] to counteract transactions intended to defeat applications under the Act.[46]

In addition to its power to vary orders for periodical payments made under the Act, the court has power under the Act to vary secured periodical payment orders made under the Matrimonial Causes Act 1973, and to vary the terms of maintenance agreements.[47]

It should be noted that, under the 1938 Act, if an applicant, for example a young child, had a good claim to maintenance in the future, the court could adjourn the proceedings.[48] Presumably this could still be done under the new Act.

Interim Orders

If an applicant is suffering hardship pending the hearing of the application, it is possible for personal representatives of the deceased to pay and the beneficiaries under the will or intestacy to consent to the payment of something "on account" of the provision which will eventually be agreed by the parties, or awarded by the court.[49] If they will not do so, then the applicant can apply for an interim order, which may be made if it appears to the court (a) that the applicant is in immediate need of financial assistance, but it is not yet possible to determine what final order (if any) should be made; and (b) that property forming part of the net estate of the deceased is or can be made available to meet the needs of the

[43] s. 6(7). An applicant will not normally be penalised for thrift: *Re Gale* [1966] Ch. 236.
[44] s. 6(9); *ante*, p. 52.
[45] ss. 10 and 11.
[46] s. 6(9).
[47] ss. 16, 17. These have already been mentioned: see *ante*, p. 19.
[48] *Re Franks* [1948] Ch. 62; *Re Bateman* (1941) 85 S.J. 454.
[49] Personal representatives would be unwise to make any such payment without the consent of all the beneficiaries or an indemnity.

applicant.[50] Interim relief is not restricted to periodical payments, but may be by way of a lump sum. However, presumably periodical payments will be more suitable than a lump sum in most cases. So far as the urgency of the case admits, the court must in making an interim order have regard to the guidelines prescribed for orders generally,[51] and the court has its general powers as to the form of orders and the burden of orders.[52] It is unlikely that applications for interim orders will be frequent. The court will be unlikely to consider such an application until all parties have had an opportunity of filing evidence; by then the court will be in a position to deal with the substantive application, if necessary on an expedited hearing.[53] An interim order is most likely to be made where, because of difficulties in administration, there is expected to be delay in ascertaining the amount of the estate.

Personal representatives and beneficiaries will naturally be reluctant to agree to interim payments unless the applicant's claim is a strong one, because the money so paid will probably be lost for ever to the estate. On the other hand, the possibility of such loss is implicit in the court's power to make interim orders.[54] Perhaps the practical answer is that an applicant who is in immediate need of financial assistance will usually have a strong claim.[55] Certainly the possibility of loss to the beneficiaries as a result of a successful applicant for an interim order having received nothing on the final hearing of his or her application does not seem to have caused trouble under the 1938 Act.

The court has the power to make interim orders of other kinds, if appropriate, for example orders for the preservation of property in its existing state.[56]

---

[50] s. 5(1).
[51] s. 5(3).
[52] s. 5(2).
[53] Appeals from interim orders are strongly discouraged: *Re Pitkin*, C.A., January 18, 1980, C.A.T. 80/19.
[54] Note the protection for personal representatives in s. 20(2). Maybe "conditions or restrictions" as mentioned in s. 5(1), can give some protection to the beneficiaries.
[55] Any interim payments ordered by the court may be treated by a final order as paid on account of the provision ordered by that final order: s. 5(4).
[56] *Re Kozdrach*, C.A., November 9, 1979, C.A.T. 79/755.

6 Property Available for Provision

The basic principle is that provision is ordered out of the "net estate" of the deceased. This is defined in the first instance[1] as (a) all property of which the deceased had power to dispose by his will[2] (otherwise than by virtue of a special power of appointment) less the amount of his funeral, testamentary and administration expenses, debts and liabilities, including any capital transfer tax payable out of his estate on his death. However, the definition is extended[3] to include (b) any property in respect of which the deceased held a general power of appointment (not being a power exercisable by will) which has not been exercised; (c) money or property passing by statutory nomination or *donatio mortis causa*; (d) property held on a joint tenancy; and (e) money or property made available as a result of the exercise by the court of its powers to set aside dispositions and contracts intended to defeat an application for family provision (these powers are discussed in the section on anti-avoidance provisions, *post*, p. 62.[4])

Property of which the Deceased had Power to Dispose

This alone was the net estate for the purposes of the 1938 Act and the 1965 Act. As part of their normal duties, the personal representatives of the deceased will have to ascertain what property the deceased owned, and any doubts must be resolved by finding out the relevant facts and applying the relevant principles of the general law. However, two problems of ownership can usefully be mentioned in connection with applications for family provision. First, there may be an item or items of property of which the deceased was the undoubted legal owner, but in which some other

---

[1] s. 25(1) "net estate" (*a*).
[2] The fact that the property passes as *bona vacantia* on the death of the deceased intestate is irrelevant: s. 24. So is the fact that the deceased lacked the capacity to make a valid will: s. 25(2).
[3] s. 25(1) "net estate" (*b*) to (*e*).
[4] *post*, pp. 62–68.

person claims rights of beneficial ownership under a trust. It should be comparatively easy to find out whether an express trust exists, but problems will arise if the alleged trust is a resulting trust,[5] arising from alleged contributions made towards the purchase price or cost of repair or improvement of the item of property.[6] Secondly, there may be an item of property—for example, the home of the deceased—in respect of which a person may assert a contractual claim, usually based upon a contract to make a will.[7]

These problems of ownership can arise when there is no application for family provision, but they are especially relevant to such applications because an applicant may make a claim by way of contract or resulting trust in addition to or in the alternative to an application for family provision. Also a beneficiary, faced with an application for family provision, may seek to reduce the net estate by making such a claim. An obvious example of the latter situation would be the mistress who asserts that she helped to pay for the house in which she lived with the deceased. Claims must be assessed on their individual merits, but those based on contract will be subject to the anti-avoidance provisions discussed below.[8]

Powers of Appointment

Since a general power of appointment *inter vivos* or by will allows the donee to appoint to himself, property subject to it is property of which he could dispose by will, and as such is within the net estate of the donee. However, a general power may be restricted to exercise *inter vivos*, and the Act provides that property in respect of which the deceased held such a power, which he had not exercised, also forms part of his net estate.[9]

Special powers of appointment enable the donee to appoint property among a limited group or class of persons only. Property in respect of which the deceased had such a power does not form part of his net estate for the purposes of the Act. The deceased could never have made such property his own, therefore it was never something out of which he was under any sort of obligation to make provision of the kind with which the jurisdiction is concerned. The

---

[5] Sometimes called an implied or imputed trust.
[6] For such trusts see Snell, *Equity*, 28th ed., pp. 179–187.
[7] For such contracts, see Theobald, *Wills*, 14th ed., pp. 92–95. *Wakeham* v. *Mackenzie* [1968] 1 W.L.R. 1175; *Re Gonin* [1977] 3 W.L.R. 379. A claim might also be based on proprietary estoppel: Snell, pp. 558–563, *Inwards* v. *Baker* [1965] 2 Q.B. 29; *Jones (A.E.)* v. *Jones (F.W.)* [1977] 1 W.L.R. 438; *Greasley* v. *Cooke* [1980] 1 W.L.R. 1306; *Burns* v. *Burns* [1984] Ch. 317.
[8] *post*, pp. 62–68.
[9] s. 25(1) "net estate" (*b*).

donee's obligation is and ought to be governed by the terms of the power, and the well-established principles of law and equity relating to powers of appointment generally. Indeed, any attempt to extend the family provision jurisdiction to the exercise of special powers of appointment would create difficulties in relation to those principles, especially the principles concerning "fraud on a power."[10]

It may be doubted whether powers of appointment of any kind require extensive consideration in the context of family provision law. Problems arising from such powers are conspicuous by their absence from the reported cases.

Statutory Nominations

Some statutes and statutory instruments authorise persons who own or are entitled to certain kinds of property to dispose of it by nominations made during their lifetime but taking effect on their death.[11] The property concerned is mostly either the remuneration of public servants, or savings in public securities such as National Savings Certificates. The value of property which can be nominated in this way is restricted, usually (but not always) to a comparatively low level. The Act treats property so nominated as part of the net estate of the deceased, to the extent of its value at the death of the deceased, and after the deduction of any capital transfer tax payable in respect of it.[12]

The Act provides that no person shall be liable for having paid the sum or transferred the property nominated to the persons named in the nomination in accordance with the directions given in the nomination.[13] This measure of protection for the holder of the nominated fund, usually some sort of public office, may on the wording of the Act apply even after an order has been made, but it need not affect the result of the court order as between beneficiaries and applicants. It is submitted that successful applicants would have an equity to trace.[14]

Other nominations made by the deceased, for example under the terms of his or her employer's pension scheme, are not covered; these nominations are discussed, *post*.[15]

[10] See Snell, *Equity*, 28th ed., pp. 549–553.
[11] For a list, see Administration of Estates (Small Payments) Act 1965, Sched. 2; for monetary limits see S.I. 1984 No. 539.
[12] s. 8(1).
[13] s. 8(1).
[14] See *post*, p. 59.
[15] p. 60.

Donationes Mortis Causa[16]

The Act treats property so given as part of the net estate of the deceased, on the same terms as to capital transfer tax[17] and otherwise as property subject to a statutory nomination.[18]

Property Held on Joint Tenancy

The deceased's share in property of which he was a beneficial joint tenant will accrue to the other joint tenant or tenants on his death, and will accordingly not be property of which he or she could dispose by his or her will.[19] The Law Commission felt that this could create an unsatisfactory situation in cases where a major asset of the deceased, for example his or her dwelling-house, was held jointly.[20] The Act therefore enables the court to treat the deceased's share in such property as part of his or her estate at its value immediately before his or her death.[21] For the purposes of the Act, it is made clear that there can be a joint tenancy of a chose in action,[22] for example, the asset represented by a credit balance in a joint bank account.

In contrast to the provisions relating to statutory nominations and *donationes mortis causa*, the deceased's share under a joint tenancy is not automatically treated as part of his estate for the purpose of the Act; the court has to make an order to that effect. Moreover, the application for provision under which the order is made must have been commenced before the expiry of the general six-month time limit for applications. The court's discretion to extend this general time limit does not allow it to dispense with this requirement in relation to property held on a joint tenancy.[23]

In determining the extent to which the deceased's beneficial share is to be treated as part of the net estate, the court is directed to have regard to any capital transfer tax payable in respect of that share.[24]

If the court does make an order treating the share as part of the net estate, the share will not be treated differently from the rest of the net estate, merely by virtue of being joint property.[25]

---

[16] Williams, Mortimer and Sunnucks, pp. 531 *et seq.*
[17] s. 8(2).
[18] see s. 8(3).
[19] Megarry and Wade, *The Law of Real Property*, 5th ed., 1984, pp. 417, 432; contrast property held by beneficial tenants in common.
[20] Law Comm. 61, para. 138.
[21] s. 9; for some conveyancing aspects, see [1980] Conv. 60.
[22] s. 9(4).
[23] s. 9(1).
[24] s. 9(2).
[25] *Re Crawford* (1983) 4 F.L.R. 273.

When the court makes an order treating the share as part of the net estate, nobody is made liable for anything done before the order was made.[26] Thus a bank can safely pay the balance in a joint bank account to the survivor of the joint holders. Moreover, the surviving joint tenant must himself, it is submitted, be able to dispose of the property without incurring any liability. In that event, the applicant would presumably have the right to trace the property or its proceeds in equity.[27]

Property Available as a Result of the Anti-Avoidance Provisions in the Act

The anti-avoidance provisions are considered as a whole in the section, *post*.[28] If money or property is recovered under these provisions, then by that very fact it becomes available for provision.

Property not Available: Insurance Policies

The deceased may have insured his life for the benefit of himself or his estate, creating no trust of the proceeds of the policy. In that the event the proceeds of the policy will be part of his estate when he dies, and liable to be made the subject of an order under the Act. If the deceased created a trust of the policy, for example for the benefit of his wife, the proceeds of the policy will not fall into his estate.[29] The Act leaves this situation untouched, although the payment by the deceased of the premium or premiums under a policy of either kind is capable of being a disposition intended to defeat an application for provision, and is therefore subject to the anti-avoidance provisions: see the section on anti-avoidance provisions, *post*.[30]

If an applicant for provision or a beneficiary of the estate is also the beneficiary under a trust policy, then the benefit under the policy would presumably be part of the financial resources of that applicant or beneficiary, and would thereby fall to be considered by

---

[26] s. 9(3).

[27] See Williams, Mortimer and Sunnucks, p. 974; *Snell, Equity*, 28th ed., 1982, pp. 295–303, Goff and Jones, *The Law of Restitution*, 2nd ed., 1978, pp. 46 *et seq.* For a comment on the problems that can arise, see [1980] Conv. 60.

[28] pp. 62–68, *post*.

[29] See s. 11 of the Married Women's Property Act 1882.

[30] pp. 62–68, *post*. The report of the Law Commission appears to assume that the act of creating a trust of a policy is not a disposition of property within s. 10. See Law Comm. 61, paras. 203–206. It is not clear why it should not be, especially if the policy existed before the trust was created.

the court under the general guidelines, so as to affect the order made on an application.[31]

Property not Available: Non Statutory Nominations

The major source of provision for the family of a deceased person may be neither the property he owns, nor the benefits he has himself arranged with an independent insurance company, but the benefits payable under a pension scheme run by his employers. Moreover, this source of provision may well become more important in the future, as occupational pension schemes continue to spread. The benefits under a scheme may under the rules of the scheme fall automatically into the estate of the deceased employee, in which case they will be property of which he or she was competent to dispose, and as such be part of the net estate available for provision under the Act. Alternatively, they may, under the rules of the scheme, be automatically payable to another person or persons, for example a surviving spouse, in which case they will not be part of the net estate of the deceased. However, schemes commonly give the employee a power of nomination, under which the employee can name the person he wishes to take the benefit payable under the scheme. The legal nature and effect of such nominations have not been fully worked out.[32] A nomination may be binding on the trustees of the scheme, or (as is more usual) it may merely take effect as a request; this will depend upon the true interpretation of the scheme, but in either case the money which is paid under the scheme would seem to be no part of the net estate of the deceased as defined in the Act. Even if the nomination is binding on the trustees, the money payable under it is unlikely to be "property of which the deceased had power to dispose *by his will*."[33]

As with insurance policies subject to a trust, if an applicant for provision or a beneficiary of the estate is also the beneficiary under a nomination, then the benefit must be part of the financial resources of the person concerned, which falls to be considered by the court under the general guidelines.[34] But this will not help much if the estate is small, and the money payable under the nomination is the most substantial source out of which the deceased could have made provision for his family and dependants. Under the Act, if a man with an estate of £25,000 leaves £5,000 to his wife and £20,000

[31] See *Re Charman* [1951] 2 T.L.R. 1095, and *Re Lecoche* (1967) 111 S.J. 136; and see p. 28 *ante*.
[32] *Re Danish Bacon Co. Ltd. Staff Pension Fund Trusts* [1971] 1 W.L.R. 248; (1967) 31 Conv. (N.S.) 85 (Samuels).
[33] s. 25(1) "net estate" (*a*); *Re Cairnes* (1982) 12 Fam. Law 177.
[34] *Re Lecoche, ante*.

to his mistress, the wife can apply for provision; but if a man with an estate of £5,000 leaves it all to his wife, but nominates a death benefit of £20,000 to his mistress, the court is powerless. This seems anomalous.

The Law Commission recognised the problem,[35] but made the point that the trustees of pension funds generally have a discretion, and they can confidently be expected to act conscientiously. There is force in this, but it does not remove the anomaly. The question whether nominations under pension funds should be subject to the powers of the court under the Act can be argued both ways, as the Law Commission recognised. Maybe the right answer depends upon which of the two different sentiments on which the Act can be said to be based is the more important.[36] To the extent that the basis of the Act is a sentiment that family and dependants ought to be left money to live on, benefits under nominations should be subject to the Act. But to the extent that the basis is a sentiment that family and dependants have the primary right to the deceased's property, then the case for bringing benefits under nominations within the Act is less clear, because such benefits were never the property of the deceased.

[35] Law Comm. 61, paras. 143, 213.
[36] See p. 8, *ante.*

7 Anti-Avoidance Provisions

One of the main criticisms, if not the main criticism, of the 1938 Act was the ease with which it could be avoided.[1] By disposing of property before his death, a person could put that property out of the reach of an order for family provision. The disposal did not even have to deprive the disponor of all enjoyment of the property, because he could reserve rights in it for himself during his life, by way of a life interest or, in the case of real property, a lease. There did not even have to be an immediate disposal, because a mere contract to dispose of specific property, or of a share in residue, by will, could frustrate an application for provision. The contract had the effect of reducing the net estate of the deceased, and thus the property available for provision.[2]

The new Act modifies this unsatisfactory situation. There are two sets of provisions, those in section 10 relating to dispositions, and those in section 11 relating to contracts to leave property by will; sections 12 and 13 contain supplementary provisions for both. The sections do not operate in quite the same way; nor do they operate in the same manner as the anti-avoidance section (s. 37) of the Matrimonial Causes Act 1973, although their objective is similar. The sections do not enable the court to set aside dispositions and contracts directly. Instead they enable it to order a person who has benefited under certain dispositions and contracts made by the deceased to help provide the resources from which claims to family provision can be satisfied. Such a person will of course have to be made a defendant in the proceedings.

It should be noted that the powers which the sections give are only available when an application is made for provision, and not, for example, when an application is made to vary an existing order for periodical payments.[3]

---

[1] Tyler, pp. 24–28.
[2] For contracts to make a will, see n. 7 on p. 56, *ante*. The Privy Council cases of *Schaefer* v. *Schuhmann* [1972] A.C. 572 and *Dillon* v. *Public Trustee of New Zealand* [1941] A.C. 294 (disapproved in *Schaefer* v. *Schuhmann*) and *Cadogan* v. *Cadogan* [1977] 1 W.L.R. 1041 may be relevant to questions of avoidance when ss. 10 and 11 of the new Act do not apply.
[3] s. 6(9).

Dispositions

The court is given power to order a donee, whether or not he still holds any interest in the property disposed of to him, to provide for the purposes of making financial provision such sum of money, or other property, as may be specified in the order. Before exercising this power, the court must be satisfied (a) that, less than six years before the death of the deceased, he made a disposition with the intention of defeating an application for financial provision under the Act; (b) that full valuable consideration[4] was not given for the disposition; and (c) that the exercise of the power would facilitate the making of financial provision for the applicant.[5] The requirement of intention is satisfied if the court is of the opinion that, on a balance of probabilities, the intention of the deceased, though not necessarily his sole intention, was to impede an order for financial provision under the Act.[6] In deciding whether and how to exercise its powers under the section, the court is directed to have regard to the circumstances in which the disposition was made, any valuable consideration given for the disposition, the relationship (if any) of the donee to the deceased, the conduct and financial resources of the donee, and all the other circumstances of the case.[7]

For the purposes of this section, "disposition" includes any payment of money (including an assurance premium) and any conveyance, assurance, appointment or gift of property of any description, whether made by an instrument or otherwise. However, there are expressly excluded (a) any provision in a will, any statutory nomination, and any *donatio mortis causa* and (b) any appointment of property made, otherwise than by will, in the exercise of a special power of appointment.[8] The section does not apply to any disposition made before the commencement of the Act.[9]

The donee is given a measure of protection, in two ways. First, he can operate a kind of third party procedure, whereby if the disposition to him is challenged he can himself challenge other dispositions.[10] Secondly, if he was given money, he cannot be ordered to provide more in money or the value of property than the money he received; and if he was given property, he cannot be

---

[4] This does not include marriage or a promise of marriage: s. 25(1).
[5] s. 10(2).
[6] s. 12(1); *Re Kennedy* [1980] C.L.Y. 2820, County Court.
[7] s. 10(6); for s. 10 generally, see [1978] Conv. 13.
[8] s. 10(7).
[9] s. 10(8).
[10] s. 10(5). The same subsection gives similar rights to any applicant for an order under s. 2 of the Act. It is not clear what this adds to the rights already conferred on such persons by s. 10(1) and (2).

ordered to provide more than the value of that property at the death of the deceased (or, if he had already disposed of the property by that time, its value when he disposed of it).[11]

The section appears to imply that an order can be made against a donee for the benefit of an applicant even if the disposition to that donee was made with the intention of defeating an application by some other person. Thus, if the donee is a mistress, and the disposition to her was made to defeat an application by a wife, the court could make an order against her for the benefit of the deceased's children.

Contracts

The provisions as to contracts are necessarily somewhat different, although the approach is the same. The court has to be satisfied on four points: (a) that the deceased made a contract by which he agreed to leave or transfer money or property by will; (b) that the contract was made with the intention of defeating an application for financial provision under the Act; (c) that full valuable consideration[12] was not given or promised by the donee or anyone else and (d) that the exercise of the court's powers under the section would facilitate the making of financial provision for the applicant.[13] If the court is so satisfied, it may, if money has been paid or property transferred under the contract, direct the donee to provide money or other property for the purpose of making financial provision. If and in so far as money has not been paid or property has not been transferred, the court may direct the personal representatives not to pay or transfer it.[14]

The intention of the deceased under point (b) is a matter of the balance of probabilities, but if there was no valuable consideration for the contract, the intention is presumed until the contrary is shown.[15]

As with dispositions, the powers relating to contracts are discretionary; even if the court is satisfied on the four points, it may nevertheless refuse to make an order. In deciding whether to make an order, and in deciding what kind of order to make, the court is directed, as with dispositions, to have regard to the circumstances in which the contract was made, the relationship of the donee to the deceased, the conduct and financial resources of the donee and all

---

[11] s. 10(3), (4). Allowance is made for any capital transfer tax paid by the donee.
[12] This does not include marriage or a promise of marriage: s. 25(1).
[13] s. 11(2).
[14] s. 11(2).
[15] s. 12(1), (2).

the circumstances of the case.[16] The donee is protected by a provision that the court shall exercise its powers only to the extent that the money or the value of the property given exceeds the value of any valuable consideration for the contract.[17] Contracts made before the commencement of the Act are not caught.[18]

It should be noted that a contract can be the subject of an order under section 11 however long before the death of the deceased it was made; there is no time limit, as there is for dispositions. The reason for this distinction is that the deceased will generally have retained enjoyment of the money or property subject to the contract up until the time of his death.[19]

Personal Representatives

The anti-avoidance provisions in sections 10 and 11 are available against the personal representatives of the donee as they are against the donee, but once the donee's property has been distributed by his personal representatives it is no longer subject to the provisions.[20] Moreover, personal representatives are not liable if they distribute any of the donee's property without notice of the making of an application under sections 10 or 11.[21]

Trustees

If the disposition or contract involves the payment of money or transfer of property to a trustee, any order made against the trustee cannot take from him more than the money, or the value of the property, that he has at the date of the order.[22] In addition, the trustee cannot be made liable for distributing money or property on the ground that he ought to have taken into account the possibility of an application under sections 10 or 11 being made.[23]

---

[16] s. 11(4).
[17] s. 11(3).
[18] s. 11(6), April 1, 1976.
[19] Law Comm. 61, para. 237.
[20] s. 12(4).
[21] s. 13(1). But they are allowed to anticipate the making of an application and delay the performance of a contract which may be the subject of an order under s. 11: see s. 20(3).
[22] s. 13(1). Note the terms of the subsection—property which is derived from the money and property transferred is caught.
[23] s. 13(2).

The Desirability of Anti-Avoidance Provisions

The Report of the Law Commission discusses the arguments for and against anti-avoidance provisions at some length.[24] The Commission accepted that there were arguments against such provisions. Gifts are often made to preserve the family fortune from the effects of capital taxation, and such gifts ought not to be challenged; it is often difficult to determine the true intention of the deceased; there is little evidence of any widespread mischief; the powers would be ineffective and could be avoided, for example by the purchase of an annuity; and attempts to prevent evasion can lead to great complication. However, balancing these arguments against the importance of ensuring that family provision laws are effective (which it considered overriding), the Law Commission recommended the scheme embodied in the Act. It is submitted that this was right. Measures to avoid the 1938 and the 1965 Acts do appear to have been taken by some testators,[25] and the anti-avoidance provisions of the new Act should stop the worst examples.

The anti-avoidance provisions as they stand will not prevent some degree of avoidance. For example, a disposition of property made more than six years before the death of the deceased will not be caught at all, and a gift of the proceeds of an insurance policy will only be caught as to the premiums paid by the deceased within six years of his death.[26] But in both cases the donor will probably have to keep something for himself to live on, so there will be at least some estate against which an order can be made. Perhaps the most effective form of avoidance is that which could be practised by a man or woman who has an income ceasing on death, for example a pension or an annuity, and an estate largely made up of a dwelling-house. The dwelling-house could be transferred to the person whom the transferor wished to benefit in return for a long lease terminable on death, and provided that the transferor lived for six years afterwards his or her estate would be greatly reduced, and the anti-avoidance provisions would be frustrated. Instead of a lease terminable on death, a life interest could be created, to produce the same result.

A discretionary trust might also be effective to avoid the Act, provided it was set up at least six years before the death of the settlor. The trustees would have to be selected with care, especially

[24] Law Comm. 61, paras. 189–197.
[25] For a precedent of a settlement, see (1944) 9 Conv. (N.S.) 282, and for an example of avoidance in the matrimonial jurisdiction, see *Cadogan* v. *Cadogan* [1977] 1 W.L.R. 1041.
[26] But see n. 30, on p. 59, *ante*.

if the settlor wished them to apply part of the settled funds for his benefit during his life.

Court Approval

It was suggested to the Law Commission that a person ought to be able during his lifetime to secure the approval of the court to a transaction in order that it might not be impugned in family provision proceedings after his death. The Law Commission did not accept this suggestion.[27] Its view was that: "The proposed powers are aimed at cases where there was clearly an intention to defeat a possible application. It would be difficult, if not impossible, for the court to decide whether to approve a particular transaction without going into all the circumstances of the case and, possibly, hearing all interested parties. This would be a cumbersome procedure to invoke as a safeguard against a possible application for family provision. There might be a case for a provision preventing an applicant from questioning a transaction to which he or she had consented in writing. We think this is unnecessary as the court would be hardly likely to reopen a transaction for the benefit of any applicant who had consented to it."[28] The point made by the Law Commission about consent in writing has some force, but it is arguable that the Commission dismissed the suggestion of court approval too readily. The anti-avoidance provisions may be aimed at cases where there was clearly an intention to defeat a possible application, but the existence of such an intention may be very unclear until it is established or rebutted in court proceedings. It is the uncertainty created by the anti-avoidance provisions that works the mischief. Moreover, the point about the cumbersome nature of any procedure for court approval looks implausible. The procedure could simply enable the court to make a finding of fact as to the intention of the donor, which would have the status of any other finding of fact made in court proceedings.

The power to make such a finding of fact might be useful, not only in proceedings taken especially to obtain it, but also in other proceedings. It is at least possible that a disposition or contract which had been carried out pursuant to court approval of some kind granted under some other jurisdiction, for example, under the Variation of Trusts Act 1958, could be the subject of challenge

---

[27] Law Comm. 61, paras. 220, 221.
[28] How does this relate to the principle that the jurisdiction of the court under the Act cannot be ousted by private agreement? The answer probably lies in the distinction between consent as an absolute bar to an application and consent as a factor influencing the court against making an order. See also p. 19, *ante.*

under sections 10 and 11. An express power in the court to make a finding of fact as to the donee's intention at the time of the disposition or contract, available in any kind of proceedings, could prevent such an unsatisfactory state of affairs.

8 Jurisdiction and Procedure

An application for an order under the Act may be made in the Chancery Division of the High Court, the Family Division of the High Court, or the county court.

Chancery and Family Divisions

The procedure on an application under the Act in the High Court is regulated by Order 99 of the Rules of the Supreme Court.[1] This order allows the applicant to bring proceedings either in the Chancery Division or the Family Division, at his option.[2] It is submitted that this dual jurisdiction is desirable, because some applications are more suitable for the Chancery Division, and some for the Family Division. The Law Commission was given[3] the following examples of those more suitable for the Chancery Division:

   (a) applications in which it is necessary for a Chancery judge to decide in a probate action on the validity of the will which is alleged not to make reasonable provision for the applicant. In such cases the probate action can be heard immediately before the family provision application, and by the same judge, thus saving time and expense;

   (b) applications in which a Chancery judge must first decide the true meaning of the will on a construction summons.[4] In these cases also the construction summons can be heard immediately before the family provision application and by the same judge;

   (c) those in which problems arise in the administration of the estate of the deceased either as a result of or independently of the application for family provision;

[1] See App. 2, *post.*

[2] In 1977, 231 originating summonses were issued in the Chancery Division in London, and 178 in the Chancery Division outside London. 76 were issued in the Family Division in London, and 51 in the Family Division outside London. In 1984, 130 were issued in the Chancery Division in London, and 124 in the Family Division in London. 181 were issued in the Family Division outside London, but the Chancery Division figures for outside London are not available.

[3] See Law Comm. 61, para. 253.

[4] Other documents may have to be construed: *Re Lidington* [1940] Ch. 927.

(d) those in which preliminary orders are required to ascertain or safeguard the assets of the estate. In connection with the safeguarding of the assets, the speed of the interlocutory Chancery procedure on motion, which brings a matter before the judge in open court after only two clear days' notice, may be especially valuable;

(e) those in which complicated accounts have to be taken;

(f) those in which an order for family provision might have important tax implications; this particularly applies, of course, to applications against the larger estates.

To these must now be added, it is suggested, applications in which a Chancery Judge is asked to rectify a Will[5] and the rectification, if granted, will affect the application for family provision.

On the other hand, some cases are more suitable for the Family Division, for example, perhaps, those in which there has already been an order under the Matrimonial Causes Act 1973 or its predecessors.[6] Moreover, the greater similarity between the family provision jurisdiction and the matrimonial jurisdiction brought about by the new Act must make the Family Division a more appropriate forum than it was before.

In many if not most cases, both divisions will be equally suitable, and the practitioner's choice between them can quite properly depend upon his own inclination. In any event, the jurisdictions of the two divisions have been connected for a long time, especially in relation to wills and the welfare of children.[7] Many practitioners in the one division have appeared happily in the other, and for some years now counsel practising in the Chancery Division have been appointed judges of the Family Division. The new Act will strengthen the connection between the divisions, as will the increasing importance of the financial and property aspects of divorce.

If two points on all this may be emphasised, they are that practitioners in one of the divisions must be prepared to go into the other, and that the expertise available in the two divisions must be both sought and offered in order to solve common problems. This applies especially to the common problems of property law, finance, and taxation.

---

[5] Under s. 20 of the Administration of Justice Act 1982.

[6] See *Practice Note* [1976] 1 W.L.R. 418. Details of such proceedings should be given in the affidavit in support of the summons.

[7] Probate, Will Construction, and Wardship.

High Court Procedure

The procedure on an application in the High Court is the same in the Chancery Division as in the Family Division. Perhaps the most significant feature of the procedure is that masters of the Chancery Division, registrars of the Principal Registry of the Family Division, and district registrars may hear applications, and make final orders for disposing of them. This is the effect of rule 8 of Order 99, which provides that proceedings under the Act may be disposed of in chambers. No doubt masters and registrars will exercise their discretion so as to refer to a judge any case which is likely to involve a difficult, long or complex issue of fact or law[8] or a question of jurisdiction, but no doubt also they will be the effective tribunal of decision in many if not most cases. This should save time and expense. There is a power to transfer applications to the county court (r. 11), but this may be seldom exercised: see the discussion of the county court jurisdiction *post*, p. 79.

The application has to be made by originating summons in the expedited form (Form No. 10 in App. A to the Rules of the Supreme Court), supported by an affidavit (r. 3).[9] If an extension of time for making the application is sought under section 4, this should be expressly asked for in the originating summons, and the grounds on which it is claimed should be set out in the affidavit in support.[10] Though it is not required by any rule or practice direction, it is also desirable to ask expressly in the originating summons for any provision claimed out of property treated as part of the net estate by virtue of sections 8 and 9,[11] or any relief sought under the anti-avoidance provisions.[12] Rule 3(3) states that the affidavit should be lodged with the court, and should exhibit an official copy of the grant of representation to the deceased's estate and every testamentary document admitted to proof. In some cases, the applicant may not have these documents, but it should be possible to obtain them from the Probate Registry. Indeed, the applicant may not have time to prepare his affidavit before the six months' time limit under section 4 of the Act has expired. In these situations, it is suggested that the applicant should issue the summons and leave the lodging of the affidavit until it is ready. If necessary, the affidavit will have to explain why copies cannot be exhibited as required by the rule. A copy of the applicant's affidavit must be served on every defendant, with the summons (r. 3(3)).

---

[8] See *Re Beaumont* [1980] Ch. 444.
[9] For the position if there is no grant, see p. 11, *ante.*
[10] *Practice Note* [1976] 1 W.L.R. 418; *post*, App. 2.
[11] pp. 52–59, *ant.*
[12] ss. 10–13, *supra*, pp. 62–68.

The affidavit lodged on behalf of the applicant should contain full information about the applicant and about such of the circumstances of the case as are relevant to the statutory guidelines. In particular the affidavit should state the effect of the deceased's will (or of the intestacy rules) and the resources and needs of the applicant. This statement of resources and needs can conveniently be made as a "budget," showing income and outgoings (and also the capital possessed by the applicant, if any).[13]

Rule 5 provides that within 21 days any defendant who is a personal representative must, and any other defendant may, lodge an affidavit in answer. By rule 5(2), the affidavit in answer lodged by a personal representative must state, to the best of his ability: (a) full particulars of the value of the deceased's net estate; (b) the person or classes of persons beneficially interested in the estate, giving the names and (in the case of those who are not already parties) the addresses of all living beneficiaries, and the value of their interests so far as ascertained; (c) if such be the case, that any living beneficiary (naming him) is a minor or a patient within the meaning of Order 80, r. 1 of the Rules of the Supreme Court; and (d) any facts known to the personal representative which might affect the exercise of the court's powers under the Act.[14] Every defendant who lodges an affidavit must serve copies of it on the other parties (except those represented by the same solicitor as himself) (r. 5(3)).

The defendants or any of them are entitled to apply to strike out an application either under Order 18, rule 19 of the Rules of the Supreme Court, or under the inherent jurisdiction of the Court, on the ground that it discloses no reasonable cause of action; or it is scandalous, frivolous or vexatious; or is otherwise an abuse of the process of the Court. In appropriate cases, such an application may be a convenient way of deciding a preliminary question which has no connection with the merits of the application, for example a question as to domicile or parentage. However, applications to strike out are unlikely to save time or costs for defendants on the question whether an applicant under paragraph (e) was maintained by the deceased. In this connection the Court of Appeal has expressed the view that claims under the Act ought to be dealt with

---

[13] If necessary, the affidavit should also adduce evidence of the relationship which entitles the applicant to apply (see n. 2 on p. 16, *ante*), and the grounds of any claim under ss. 8 and 9, or under the anti-avoidance provisions (ss. 10–13).

[14] A personal representative who is also a beneficiary need not disclose his means: *Re Clark* [1981] C.L.Y. 2884.

immediately on the merits, and time and money not spent on applications to strike out.[15]

Parties

Once an application has been made, further parties may have to be added. The court has its general powers as to parties under Order 15 of the Rules of the Supreme Court, and by rule 4(2) of Order 99 its power to make representation orders under Order 15, r. 13, is extended to applications under the Act. In addition, without prejudice to its general powers under Order 15, the court has power to add a person as a party or to direct that notice of the proceedings be served on him (r. 4(1)). There is also provision for the separate representation of joint applicants (r. 6), although the old practice whereby different plaintiffs were made into defendants may well be followed by the court. These procedural matters will be decided by the master or registrar at the preliminary hearings of the summons.

Because there may be argument over how the burden of any order is to be borne between existing beneficiaries,[16] it is not considered appropriate for the personal representatives to represent the beneficiaries under Order 15, r. 14. Unless there are grounds for seeking a representation order, the applicant should generally at the outset join as defendants, in addition to the personal representatives, all beneficiaries and other persons likely to be affected: this would not normally include legatees for small sums. It is likely to cause extra expense and delay if further parties have to be joined on the direction of the court, and the costs thrown away may have to be borne by the applicant.

Hearsay Evidence

The general rules relating to hearsay evidence apply to proceedings under the Act as they do to all other legal proceedings. Under the Civil Evidence Act 1968, oral or written statements made by a person can be admitted as evidence of any fact of which direct oral evidence by him would be admissible. There is some doubt whether this rule is apt to render statements of a deceased person admissible in proceedings which by their nature could only be brought after his death, so section 21 of the Act expressly provides that such statements by the deceased against whose estate the application is made are admissible under the Civil Evidence Act.

[15] *Re Dymott* C.A., December 12, 1980; C.A.T. 80/942. See also *Re Beaumont* [1980] Ch. 444.
[16] See *ante*, p. 51.

Compromise

Neither the Act nor Order 99 provides specifically for the compromise of applications but in all cases the possibility of compromising the application should be considered.[17] Although unjustified claims will no doubt be resisted by the beneficiaries and their advisers, it is difficult to say with certainty that any claim is unjustified, at least until all the evidence is lodged.[18] The saving in costs that a compromise can bring should always be borne in mind, especially when the estate is small. In negotiating a compromise, care must be taken to make use of tax law to the best advantage; the most obvious example is the total capital transfer tax exemption given to surviving spouses, which can be used to reduce the net cost of provision for a surviving spouse, and thus facilitate a compromise.

If an application under the 1938 Act was compromised, and all the parties, being of full age and capacity, embodied the compromise in a "Tomlin Order," that order was not an order made under the Act.[19] The position is the same under the 1975 Act, at least in the Chancery Division.[20] However, it is not clear what if any significance this has. Formerly, it might have been important because there was doubt whether a consent order modified the dispositions made by the will for the purposes of capital transfer tax, as an order not made by consent clearly did: see section 19(1) of the 1975 Act, and section 122 of the Finance Act 1976. However, section 146(8) of the Capital Transfer Tax Act 1984[21] now provides that, where an order is made staying or dismissing proceedings under the Act on terms set out in or scheduled to the order, section 146 has effect as if any of the terms which could have been included in an order under section 2 or section 10 of the Act were provisions of such an order.

If a charity is a beneficiary, the Attorney-General can authorise the charity to compromise an application, or the court or the Attorney-General can authorise an ex-gratia payment by the charity.[22]

---

[17] For compromise generally, see *Atkin's* Court Forms, Vol. 12 *Compromise and Settlement*; Foskett, *the Law and Practice of Compromise*.

[18] The affidavit procedure is of course helpful to and encourages compromise because the relevant evidence is available on oath before trial.

[19] Direction to Farwell J. dated April 23, 1942.

[20] *Practice Direction* [1979] 1 W.L.R. 1, which provides that memoranda of consent orders must nevertheless be endorsed, see *post*, p. 77.

[21] Re-enacting s. 122(7A) of the Finance Act 1976, which was itself inserted in s. 122 by s. 92 of the Finance Act 1980.

[22] *Re Snowden* [1970] Ch. 700.

Persons Under Disability: Minors and Patients[23]

An applicant or a beneficiary may be under disability as a minor or a mental patient. In accordance with the general rule, such a person will sue by his next friend and defend by his guardian *ad litem*. Next friends and guardians *ad litem* have a heavy responsibility, and if a compromise is proposed they must seriously consider whether it is for the benefit of the persons they have to protect.[24] Their legal advisers must consider carefully whether it is, and advise them accordingly.[25]

Order 80, rule 10 of the Rules of the Supreme Court provides that, where in any proceedings money is claimed by or on behalf of a person under disability, no settlement, compromise or payment and no acceptance of money paid into Court, whenever entered into or made, shall so far as it relates to that person's claim be valid without the approval of the Court. This rule is commonly assumed to apply to applications by minors or patients under the 1975 Act. Certainly the author of this book has never known or heard of a case in which the relevance of Order 80 has been challenged, still less of one in which a Master, Registrar or Judge has declined jurisdiction to approve the compromise of an application by a minor or patient. However, it is arguable that in strictness Order 80, rule 10 does not apply, because claims under the legislation are not claims of the payment of money, but claims to be put in the position of a legatee.[26] It is submitted that this argument is probably correct.

Apart from Order 80, rule 10, it is submitted that the Court has an inherent jurisdiction to approve a compromise of any kind on behalf of a minor or patient[26a], possibly by virtue of the *parens patriae* of the Crown. Certainly Court approval is desirable or in practice essential in the great majority of cases involving minors or patients, for the protection of other parties, and for the protection of the next friend or guardian *ad litem*, because minors and patients cannot fully bind themselves by contract. The distinction is one between a positive provision of the Rules of the Supreme Court, and the availability of an inherent jurisdiction which must usually be invoked to cure an incapacity at common law.

In the great majority of cases the distinction has no significance. However, it may have some significance in the class of case in which

---

[23] The Court of Protection may be involved; its function is to protect and control the administration of the property and affairs of persons who, through mental disorder, are incapable of managing their own affairs. See Heywood and Massey, *Court of Protection Practice*, 11th ed., 1985.

[24] *Re Whittall* [1973] 1 W.L.R. 1027.

[25] *Re Barbour's Settlement Trusts* [1974] 1 W.L.R. 1198.

[26] *Re Jennery* [1967] Ch. 280.

[26a] *Chapman v. Chapman* [1954] A.C. 429, 445.

the estate is small, and a minor or patient is a party to, but is not playing the leading part in, the litigation. An example might be a claim by a former wife in which her children, the step-children of the deceased, are also claiming as children of the family under paragraph (*d*) of subsection 1(1). If their claim is obviously secondary to that of their mother, and a quick and simple compromise can be achieved between their mother and the beneficiaries, the compromise could include a small payment to them, and Court approval dispensed with on terms that their mother gives the executors and beneficiaries an indemnity against any future claims of theirs. If Order 80, rule 10 does not apply, an arrangement of this kind is probably less vulnerable than it would be if the rule does apply. For example, the childrens' mother cannot subsequently argue that the rule invalidates her indemnity. When the Court approves a compromise it will require to have before it an affidavit by the next friend or guardian *ad litem*, deposing that he considers the proposed compromise to be for the benefit of his minor or patient, and exhibiting his solicitor's case to counsel and counsel's opinion in favour of the proposed compromise.[27]

A court order approving a compromise affecting a minor or patient is an order under the Act.

The Substantive Hearing

After the preliminary hearings of the summons, usually two in number, before the master or registrar, the summons will be adjourned to the substantive hearing.

This hearing will follow the normal course of the substantive hearing of an originating summons, whether it is in chambers or in court. The applicant's advocate will open his case and read his evidence, and then the person who has made his affidavit will be cross-examined, if orders for cross-examination have been made.[28] Then the defendants' advocates will read their evidence, and the makers of their affidavits will be cross-examined in their turn, if the appropriate orders for cross-examination have been made. Independent personal representatives, if there are such, will be represented. It is their duty to take up a neutral position, and to assist the court generally. After the evidence, there will be final speeches and judgment.

If the hearing was before a master or registrar sitting in chambers,

---

[27] *Supreme Court Practice* 1985, notes to rr. 10 and 11 of Ord. 80.
[28] There must be cross-examination if the court is to make findings on disputed questions of fact: *Re Singer* [1967] 1 W.L.R. 1482, 1485. Any necessary orders for cross-examination should be made at the preliminary hearings of the summons. See *Practice Direction* [1969] 1 W.L.R. 983.

a dissatisfied party can appeal to the judge.[29] An appeal lies from the judge to the Court of Appeal in the normal way. If the initial hearing was before the judge or before a master or registrar sitting in open court under Order 30, r. 9, then an appeal lies to the court of Appeal.[30]

The Order

Order 99, r. 7 provides that the personal representatives must produce to the court the grant of representation to the deceased's estate, and, if an order is made under the Act, the grant must remain in the custody of the court until a memorandum of the order has been endorsed on or permanently annexed to the grant. It is now the practice, both in the Chancery Division and the Family Division, to endorse a memorandum of all consent orders, whether or not strictly speaking made under the Act.[31] Section 19(3) of the Act provides for the endorsement or annexation of the memorandum, and by section 19(1) the order has effect as from the deceased's death for all purposes, including the purposes of capital transfer tax.[32]

The order is not an order for the payment of money, but puts the successful applicant in the position of a beneficiary, who can enforce the order by starting an administration action.[33] It is desirable that the provisions of the order should themselves be designed to take effect either as at death or as from 12 months after death (the end of the "executor's year"), otherwise difficulties may arise on administration for which the order makes no provision.

If, after an order has been made, there is a further application in respect of the same estate, that application has to be made by a summons in the original proceedings (r. 9).

Costs

Neither the Act nor Order 99 makes provision for the costs of an application. They are in the court's discretion. In the past, when an application under the 1938 Act or the 1965 Act succeeded, the practice was to order the costs of the parties generally on the

[29] Under Ord. 58 there is now an appeal to the judge in the Chancery Division, and not an adjournment to the judge. The personal representatives may not wish to appear on the appeal, in order to save costs. In that event, it is suggested that they seek the agreement of the other parties or the directions of the lower court.
[30] For the approach of the Court of Appeal, see p. 80, *post.*
[31] *Practice Direction* [1979] 1 W.L.R. 1.
[32] See also Capital Transfer Tax Act 1984, s. 146.
[33] *Re Jennery* [1967] Ch. 280.

common fund basis to be paid out of the estate.[34] Where an application failed, there was no consistent practice. Sometimes the normal rule in adverse litigation was followed, and the unsuccessful applicant had to pay the costs of the other parties[35]; sometimes no order for costs was made[36]; and sometimes, even, the applicant was awarded his costs out of the estate.[37]

There is no reason why the practice as to costs should not remain the same under the 1975 Act, and the author of this book has no reason to suppose that it is proving to be different.[38] Where an application is successful, the costs of all parties will almost invariably come out of the estate, taxed on the common fund basis if not agreed. If an application is unsuccessful the applicant will be very lucky indeed if he gets his costs out of the estate.[39] However, he may avoid having to pay the costs of the other parties if his application has some merit. The degree of merit required will depend on all the circumstances, and especially, it is submitted, upon the effect of the costs of the application on the beneficiaries. The Court will be less likely to make an unsuccessful applicant pay the defendants' costs if the burden of those costs is small in relation to the value of the estate, or possibly the means of the beneficiaries generally.

There is no provision for payment into court, but the discretion of the court as to costs may often be influenced by an offer of settlement made by one party. Such an offer may be especially useful when an applicant may have a strong claim to something more than he has been given by the will or under the intestacy, but not to as much as he is claiming. An offer by the beneficiaries may help them on the question of costs, if the court awards the applicant nothing, or even if it awards him no more than he was offered. To have an effect on costs, the offer must either be made as an open offer, or as an offer which is expressly stated to be made without prejudice to the issue as to the application but reserving the right to refer to it on the issue of costs.[40]

It should be noted that an award under the Act is a protected payment for legal aid purposes, so that the first £2,500 of money or

[34] In the absence of misconduct, trustees and personal representatives were awarded their costs on the indemnity basis appropriate to trustees as they still are: see Williams, Mortimer and Sunnucks, pp. 827–828.
[35] *Re Joslin* [1941] Ch. 200; *Re E.* [1966] 1 W.L.R. 709, 716.
[36] *Re Pugh* [1943] Ch. 387; *Re Gregory* [1970] 1 W.L.R. 1455.
[37] *Re Inns* [1947] Ch. 576; *Re MacLagen, The Times*, March 12, 1953.
[38] For a contrary view, see Tyler (ed. Oughton) at pp. 264–266.
[39] *Re Fullard* [1982] Fam. 42, 46.
[40] As to the latter, see *Calderbank* v. *Calderbank* [1976] Fam. 93, 106; *Cutts* v. *Head* [1984] Ch. 290.

property passing to a successful applicant who is legally aided is not subject to the statutory charge for the money expended by the Legal Aid Fund on the applicant's behalf.[41] The extent to which legal aid gives an advantage to applicants under the Act, as against beneficiaries who may be only a little more affluent, cannot be discussed here at any length, although it often has to be borne in mind by those advising beneficiaries. Small payments may have to be made to unmeritorious applicants in order to save costs, a predicament which Parliament cannot have intended. However, the Court of Appeal has emphasised the duty of practitioners to inform the Legal Aid authorities of the likely effect of costs on the estate,[42] and the solicitors acting for the personal representatives or for the beneficiaries are entitled to give information to those authorities with a view to persuading them to discharge, amend or revoke an applicant's Legal Aid Certificate.[43]

An order for security for costs can be obtained in appropriate circumstances, even against a party who is legally aided.[44]

The County Court

Under the 1975 Act, the county court has jurisdiction in family provision if the net value at the death of the deceased of the property of which he had power to dispose by his will does not exceed "the county court limit."[45] That limit for the purposes of the jurisdiction in family provision is currently £30,000.[46] There would appear to be no power for the parties to give the county court jurisdiction by agreement.

The limit of £30,000 will render the jurisdiction of the county court under the Act less and less important the longer it remains. This is especially so because the major asset of so many estates is the dwelling-house of the deceased, and dwelling-houses seem to rise in value continually and inevitably. The present limit must exclude many estates which include a dwelling-house in the sole ownership of the deceased. Indeed, the limit of the county court jurisdiction under the Act by reference to property of which the deceased had power to dispose interacts with the inclusion of the deceased's share in joint property for the purposes of orders under the Act to produce an anomaly. If the deceased was the joint owner of a house worth

---

[41] Legal Aid Act 1974, s. 9(6); Legal Aid (General) Regulations 1980, reg. 96.
[42] *Brill* v. *Proud* [1984] Fam. Law 59; C.A.T. 83/369.
[43] Matthews and Oulton, *Legal Aid and Advice*, p. 245.
[44] *Re Nobbs*, C.A., June 9, 1980, C.A.T. 80/372.
[45] County Courts Act 1984, s. 25.
[46] County Court Jurisdiction (Inheritance—Provision for Family and Dependants) Order 1981, (S.I. 1981 No. 1636).

£50,000, but had other assets worth less than £30,000, the county court has jurisdiction, but if he was the sole owner of a house worth £31,000, an application against his estate must be made in the High Court.

The jurisdiction of the county court under the Act will rise in the future with the county court limit, but the usefulness of any increase may be doubted. Now that masters and registrars, including of course district registrars, can hear and decide upon applications, there may be no advantage in giving the county court an enlarged jurisdiction, or indeed any jurisdiction at all. Maybe it would be best if all applications had to be begun in the High Court, but the masters and registrars had power to adjourn them either to a county court or to a High Court judge at their discretion, without reference to any limit of value.

Procedure in the county court is governed by Order 48 of the County Court Rules. The proceedings are begun by originating application. Order 48 is similar to Order 99 of the Rules of the Supreme Court, although the contents of the Originating Application are prescribed, and every defendant, and not just the personal representatives, must file an answer. The jurisdiction of each individual court has a geographical limitation.

Appeals

Appeals lie to the Court of Appeal from both the High Court and the county court, but questions under the Act are eminently a matter for the discretion of the judge at first instance, especially where there has been cross-examination and oral evidence. The Court of Appeal has repeatedly deprecated appeals in family provision cases, especially where the estate is small.[47] A party who loses an appeal is therefore more at risk for the costs in the Court of Appeal than for those at first instance.[48]

---

[47] *Re Gregory* [1970] 1 W.L.R. 1455; *Re Coventry* [1980] Ch. 461; *Re Portt*, C.A., March 25, 1980; C.A.T. 80/289; *Brill* v. *Proud* [1984] Fam. Law 59. As to review of the exercise of a discretion see *Ward* v. *James* [1966] 1 Q.B. 273, 293.
[48] See for example *Milward* v. *Shenton* [1972] 1 W.L.R. 711.

Appendix 1

Inheritance (Provision for Family and Dependants) Act 1975

(1975 c. 63)

An Act to make fresh provision for empowering the court to make orders for the making out of the estate of a deceased person of provision for the spouse, former spouse, child, child of the family or dependant of that person; and for matters connected therewith.

[12th November 1975]

Application for financial provision from deceased's estate

1.—(1) Where after the commencement of this Act a person dies domiciled in England and Wales and is survived by any of the following persons:—

(a) the wife or husband of the deceased;

(b) a former wife or former husband of the deceased who has not remarried;

(c) a child of the deceased;

(d) any person (not being a child of the deceased) who, in the case of any marriage to which the deceased was at any time a party, was treated by the deceased as a child of the family in relation to that marriage;

(e) any person (not being a person included in the foregoing paragraphs of this subsection) who immediately before the death of the deceased was being maintained, either wholly or partly, by the deceased;

that person may apply to the court for an order under section 2 of this Act on the ground that the disposition of the deceased's estate effected by his will or the law relating to intestacy, or the combination of his will and that law, is not such as to make reasonable financial provision for the applicant.

(2) In this Act "reasonable financial provision"—

(a) in the case of an application made by virtue of subsection (1)(a) above by the husband or wife of the deceased (except where the marriage with the deceased was the subject of a decree of judicial separation and at the date of death the decree was in force and the separation was continuing), means such financial provision as it would be reasonable in all the circumstances

of the case for a husband or wife to receive, whether or not that provision is required for his or her maintenance;
(b) in the case of any other application made by virtue of subsection (1) above, means such financial provision as it would be reasonable in all the circumstances of the case for the applicant to receive for his maintenance.

(3) For the purposes of subsection (1)(e) above, a person shall be treated as being maintained by the deceased, either wholly or partly, as the case may be, if the deceased, otherwise than for full valuable consideration, was making a substantial contribution in money or money's worth towards the reasonable needs of that person.

NOTE

This section states the persons entitled to apply for provision, and prescribes the different standards of provision for surviving spouses and other applicants. See pp. 16 to 25, *ante*.

Powers of court to make orders

2.—(1) Subject to the provisions of this Act, where an application is made for an order under this section, the court may, if it is satisfied that the disposition of the deceased's estate effected by his will or the law relating to intestacy, or the combination of his will and that law, is not such as to make reasonable financial provision for the applicant, make any one or more of the following orders:—

(a) an order for the making to the applicant out of the net estate of the deceased of such periodical payments and for such term as may be specified in the order;

(b) an order for the payment to the applicant out of that estate of a lump sum of such amount as may be so specified;

(c) an order for the transfer to the applicant of such property comprised in that estate as may be so specified;

(d) an order for the settlement for the benefit of the applicant of such property comprised in that estate as may be so specified;

(e) an order for the acquisition out of property comprised in that estate of such property as may be so specified and for the transfer of the property so acquired to the applicant or for the settlement thereof for his benefit;

(f) an order varying any ante-nuptial or post-nuptial settlement (including such a settlement made by will) made on the parties to a marriage to which the deceased was one of the parties, the variation being for the benefit of the surviving party to that marriage, or any child of that marriage, or any person who was treated by the deceased as a child of the family in relation to that marriage.

(2) An order under subsection (1)(*a*) above providing for the making out of the net estate of the deceased of periodical payments may provide for—

   (*a*) payments of such amount as may be specified in the order,

   (*b*) payments equal to the whole of the income of the net estate or of such portion thereof as may be so specified,

   (*c*) payments equal to the whole of the income of such part of the net estate as the court may direct to be set aside or appropriated for the making out of the income thereof of payments under this section,

or may provide for the amount of the payments or any of them to be determined in any other way the court thinks fit.

(3) Where an order under subsection (1)(*a*) above provides for the making of payments of an amount specified in the order, the order may direct that such part of the net estate as may be so specified shall be set aside or appropriated for the making out of the income thereof of those payments; but no larger part of the net estate shall be so set aside or appropriated than is sufficient, at the date of the order, to produce by the income thereof the amount required for the making of those payments.

(4) An order under this section may contain such consequential and supplemental provisions as the court thinks necessary or expedient for the purpose of giving effect to the order or for the purpose of securing that the order operates fairly as between one beneficiary of the estate of the deceased and another and may, in particular, but without prejudice to the generality of this subsection—

   (*a*) order any person who holds any property which forms part of the net estate of the deceased to make such payment or transfer such property as may be specified in the order;

   (*b*) vary the disposition of the deceased's estate effected by the will or the law relating to intestacy, or by both the will and the law relating to intestacy, in such manner as the court thinks fair and reasonable having regard to the provisions of the order and all the circumstances of the case;

   (*c*) confer on the trustees of any property which is the subject of an order under this section such powers as appear to the court to be necessary or expedient.

NOTE

This section specifies the orders which the court can make. Note especially the wide scope of subsection (4). Compare Matrimonial Causes Act 1973, ss. 23 and 24. See pp. 45 to 54, *ante*.

Matters to which court is to have regard in exercising powers under s. 2

3.—(1) Where an application is made for an order under section 2 of this Act, the court shall, in determining whether the disposition of the deceased's estate effected by his will or the law relating to intestacy, or the combination of his will and that law, is such as to make reasonable financial provision for the applicant and, if the court considers that reasonable financial provision has not been made, in determining whether and in what manner it shall exercise its powers under that section, have regard to the following matters, that is to say—

(a) the financial resources and financial needs which the applicant has or is likely to have in the foreseeable future;

(b) the financial resources and financial needs which any other applicant for an order under section 2 of this Act has or is likely to have in the foreseeable future;

(c) the financial resources and financial needs which any beneficiary of the estate of the deceased has or is likely to have in the foreseeable future;

(d) any obligations and responsibilities which the deceased had towards any applicant for an order under the said section 2 or towards any beneficiary of the estate of the deceased;

(e) the size and nature of the net estate of the deceased;

(f) any physical or mental disability of any applicant for an order under the said section 2 or any beneficiary of the estate of the deceased;

(g) any other matter, including the conduct of the applicant or any other person, which in the circumstances of the case the court may consider relevant.

(2) Without prejudice to the generality of paragraph (g) of subsection (1) above, where an application for an order under section 2 of this Act is made by virtue of section 1(1)(a) or 1(1)(b) of this Act, the court shall, in addition to the matters specifically mentioned in paragraphs (a) to (f) of that subsection, have regard to—

(a) the age of the applicant and the duration of the marriage;

(b) the contribution made by the applicant to the welfare of the family of the deceased, including any contribution made by looking after the home or caring for the family;

and, in the case of an application by the wife or husband of the deceased, the court shall also, unless at the date of death a decree of judicial separation was in force and the separation was continuing, have regard to the provision which the applicant might reasonably have expected to receive if on the day on which the deceased died the marriage, instead of being terminated by death, had been terminated by a decree of divorce.

(3) Without prejudice to the generality of paragraph (g) of subsection (1) above, where an application for an order under section 2 of this Act is made by virtue of section 1(1)(c) or 1(1)(d) of this Act, the court shall, in addition to the matters specifically mentioned in paragraphs (a) to (f) of that subsection, have regard to the manner in which the applicant was being or in which he might expect to be educated or trained, and where the application is made by virtue of section 1(1)(d) the court have also have regard—

  (a) to whether the deceased had assumed any responsibility for the applicant's maintenance and, if so, to the extent to which and the basis upon which the deceased assumed that responsibility and to the length of time for which the deceased discharged that responsibility;

  (b) to whether in assuming and discharging that responsibility the deceased did so knowing that the applicant was not his own child;

  (c) to the liability of any other person to maintain the applicant.

(4) Without prejudice to the generality of paragraph (g) of subsection (1) above, where an application for an order under section 2 of this Act is made by virtue of section 1(1)(e) of this Act, the court shall, in addition to the matters specifically mentioned in paragraphs (a) to (f) of that subsection, have regard to the extent to which and the basis upon which the deceased assumed responsibility for the maintenance of the applicant and to the length of time for which the deceased discharged that responsibility.

(5) In considering the matters to which the court is required to have regard under this section, the court shall take into account the facts as known to the court at the date of the hearing.

(6) In considering the financial resources of any person for the purposes of this section the court shall take into account his earning capacity and in considering the financial needs of any person for the purposes of this section the court shall take into account his financial obligations and responsibilities.

NOTE

This section gives the guidelines to which the court is directed to have regard. Some guidelines apply to all applicants, others only to particular categories of applicant. For the general guidelines, see pp. 26 to 32, *ante.*

Subsection (2) gives the particular guidelines for surviving spouses and former spouses. Compare the Matrimonial Causes Act 1973, s. 25(1), and see pp. 32 to 40, *ante.*

Subsection (3) gives the particular guidelines for children and persons treated as children. Compare Matrimonial Causes Act 1973, s. 25(2), and see pp. 40 to 42, *ante.*

Subsection (4) gives the particular guidelines for the new category of dependants. See pp. 42 to 44, *ante.*

Time-limit for applications

4. An application for an order under section 2 of this Act shall not, except with the permission of the court, be made after the end of the period of six months from the date on which representation with respect to the estate of the deceased is first taken out.

NOTE

See also s. 23. See pp. 11 to 14, *ante.*

Interim orders

5.—(1) Where on an application for an order under section 2 of this Act it appears to the court—

(a) that the applicant is in immediate need of financial assistance, but it is not yet possible to determine what order (if any) should be made under that section; and

(b) that property forming part of the net estate of the deceased is or can be made available to meet the need of the applicant;

the court may order that, subject to such conditions or restrictions, if any, as the court may impose and to any further order of the court, there shall be paid to the applicant out of the net estate of the deceased such sum or sums and (if more than one) at such intervals as the court thinks reasonable; and the court may order that, subject to the provisions of this Act, such payments are to be made until such date as the court may specify, not being later than the date on which the court either makes an order under the said section 2 or decides not to exercise its powers under that section.

(2) Subsections (2), (3) and (4) of section 2 of this Act shall apply in relation to an order under this section as they apply in relation to an order under that section.

(3) In determining what order, if any, should be made under this section the court shall, so far as the urgency of the case admits, have regard to the same matters as those to which the court is required to have regard under section 3 of this Act.

(4) An order made under section 2 of this Act may provide that any sum paid to the applicant by virtue of this section shall be treated to such an extent and in such manner as may be provided by that order as having been paid on account of any payment provided for by that order.

NOTE

See pp. 53 to 54, *ante.*

Variation, discharge etc. of orders for periodical payments

6.—(1) Subject to the provisions of this Act, where the court has made an order under section 2(1)(*a*) of this Act (in this section referred to as "the original order") for the making of periodical payments to any person (in this section referred to as "the original recipient"), the court, on an application under this section, shall have power by order to vary or discharge the original order or to suspend any provision of it temporarily and to revive the operation of any provision so suspended.

(2) Without prejudice to the generality of subsection (1) above, an order made on an application for the variation of the original order may—

(*a*) provide for the making out of any relevant property of such periodical payments and for such term as may be specified in the order to any person who has applied, or would but for section 4 of this Act be entitled to apply, for an order under section 2 of this Act (whether or not, in the case of any application, an order was made in favour of the applicant);

(*b*) provide for the payment out of any relevant property of a lump sum of such amount as may be so specified to the original recipient or to any such person as is mentioned in paragraph (*a*) above;

(*c*) provide for the transfer of the relevant property, or such part thereof as may be so specified, to the original recipient or to any such person as is so mentioned.

(3) Where the original order provides that any periodical payments payable thereunder to the original recipient are to cease on the occurrence of an event specified in the order (other than the remarriage of a former wife or former husband) or on the expiration of a period so specified, then, if, before the end of the period of six months from the date of the occurrence of that event or of the expiration of that period, an application is made for an order under this section, the court shall have power to make any order which it would have had power to make if the application had been made before that date (whether in favour of the original recipient or any such person as is mentioned in subsection (2)(*a*) above and whether having effect from that date or from such later date as the court may specify).

(4) Any reference in this section to the original order shall include a reference to an order made under this section and any reference in this section to the original recipient shall include a reference to any person to whom periodical payments are required to be made by virtue of an order under this section.

(5) An application under this section may be made by any of the following persons, that is to say—

(*a*) any person who by virtue of section 1(1) of this Act has applied, or would but for section 4 of this Act be entitled to apply, for an order under section 2 of this Act,

(*b*) the personal representatives of the deceased,

(*c*) the trustees of any relevant property, and

(*d*) any beneficiary of the estate of the deceased.

(6) An order under this section may only affect—

(*a*) property the income of which is at the date of the order applicable wholly or in part for the making of periodical payments to any person who has applied for an order under this Act, or

(*b*) in the case of an application under subsection (3) above in respect of payments which have ceased to be payable on the occurrence of an event or the expiration of a period, property the income of which was so applicable immediately before the occurrence of that event or the expiration of that period, as the case may be,

and any such property as is mentioned in paragraph (*a*) or (*b*) above is in subsections (2) and (5) above referred to as "relevant property".

(7) In exercising the powers conferred by this section the court shall have regard to all the circumstances of the case, including any change in any of the matters to which the court was required to have regard when making the order to which the application relates.

(8) Where the court makes an order under this section, it may give such consequential directions as it thinks necessary or expedient having regard to the provisions of the order.

(9) No such order as is mentioned in sections 2(1)(*d*), (*e*) or (*f*), 9, 10 or 11 of this Act shall be made on an application under this section.

(10) For the avoidance of doubt it is hereby declared that, in relation to an order which provides for the making of periodical payments which are to cease on the occurrence of an event specified in the order (other than the remarriage of a former wife or former husband) or on the expiration of a period so specified, the power to vary an order includes power to provide for the making of periodical payments after the expiration of that period or the occurrence of that event.

NOTE

See pp. 52 to 53, *ante.*

This power to vary only applies to orders for periodical payments. An application to vary cannot affect a part of the estate not already subject to the order for periodical payments, but it may be made by an applicant who did not apply on the occasion of the original application, and by certain other persons.

Payment of lump sums by instalments

7.—(1) An order under section 2(1)(*b*) or 6(2)(*b*) of this Act for the payment of a lump sum may provide for the payment of that sum by instalments of such amount as may be specified in the order.

(2) Where an order is made by virtue of subsection (1) above, the court shall have power, on an application made by the person to whom the lump sum is payable, by the personal representatives of the deceased or by the trustees of the property out of which the lump sum is payable, to vary that order by varying the number of instalments payable, the amount of any instalment and the date on which any instalment becomes payable.

NOTE

See p. 48, *ante.*

Property available for financial provision

Property treated as part of "net estate"

8.—(1) Where a deceased person has in accordance with the provisions of any enactment nominated any person to receive any sum of money or other property on his death and that nomination is in force at the time of his death, that sum of money, after deducting therefrom any capital transfer tax payable in respect thereof, or that other property, to the extent of the value thereof at the date of the death of the deceased after deducting therefrom any capital transfer tax so payable, shall be treated for the purposes of this Act as part of the net estate of the deceased; but this subsection shall not render any person liable for having paid that sum or transferred that other property to the person named in the nomination in accordance with the directions given in the nomination.

(2) Where any sum of money or other property is received by any person as a donatio mortis causa made by a deceased person, that sum of money, after deducting therefrom any capital transfer tax payable thereon, or that other property, to the extent of the value thereof at the date of the death of the deceased after deducting therefrom any capital transfer tax so payable, shall be treated for the purposes of this Act as part of the net estate of the deceased; but this subsection shall not render any person liable for having paid that sum or transferred that other property in order to give effect to that donatio mortis causa.

for an order under section 2 of this Act made by the first-mentioned party.

(4) Where an order made under subsection (1) above on the grant of a decree of judicial separation has come into force with respect to any party to a marriage, then, if the other party to that marriage dies while the decree is in force and the separation is continuing, the court shall not entertain any application for an order under section 2 of this Act made by the first-mentioned party.

NOTE

This section enables the court in matrimonial proceedings to prevent a future application for financial provision under the Act.
See pp. 18 to 19, *ante*. s. 15(1) was substituted by s. 8 of the Matrimonial and Family Proceedings Act, 1984.

[Restriction imposed in proceedings under Matrimonial and Family Proceedings Act 1984 on application under this Act

15A.—(1) On making an order under section 17 of the Matrimonial and Family Proceedings Act 1984 (orders for financial provision and property adjustment following overseas divorces, etc) the court, if it considers it just to do so, may, on the application of either party to the marriage, order that the other party to the marriage shall not on the death of the applicant be entitled to apply for an order under section 2 of this Act.

In this subsection "the court" means the High Court or, where a county court has jurisdiction by virtue of Part V of the Matrimonial and Family Proceedings Act 1984, a county court.

(2) Where an order under subsection (1) above has been made with respect to a party to a marriage which has been dissolved or annulled, then, on the death of the other party to that marriage, the court shall not entertain an application under section 2 of this Act made by the first-mentioned party.

(3) Where an order under subsection (1) above has been made with respect to a party to a marriage the parties to which have been legally separated, then, if the other party to the marriage dies while the legal separation is in force, the court shall not entertain an application under section 2 of this Act made by the first-mentioned party.]

NOTE

This section was added by s. 25(2) of the Matrimonial and Family Proceedings Act 1984.

Variation and discharge of secured periodical payments orders made under Matrimonial Causes Act 1973

16.—(1) Where an application for an order under section 2 of this Act is made to the court by any person who was at the time of the death of the deceased entitled to payments from the deceased under a secured periodical payments order made under the Matrimonial Causes Act 1973, then, in the proceedings on that application, the court shall have power, if an application is made under this section by that person or by the personal representative of the deceased, to vary or discharge that periodical payments order or to revive the operation of any provision thereof which has been suspended under section 31 of that Act.

(2) In exercising the powers conferred by this section the court shall have regard to all the circumstances of the case, including any order which the court proposes to make under section 2 or section 5 of this Act and any change (whether resulting from the death of the deceased or otherwise) in any of the matters to which the court was required to have regard when making the secured periodical payments order.

(3) The powers exercisable by the court under this section in relation to an order shall be exercisable also in relation to any instrument executed in pursuance of the order.

NOTE

This section enables the court in family provision proceedings to vary or discharge secured periodical payment orders made under the Matrimonial Causes Act 1973. See sections 23 and 31 of that Act, and pp. 18 to 19, *ante.*

Variation and revocation of maintenance agreements

17.—(1) Where an application for an order under section 2 of this Act is made to the court by any person who was at the time of the death of the deceased entitled to payments from the deceased under a maintenance agreement which provided for the continuation of payments under the agreement after the death of the deceased, then, in the proceedings on that application, the court shall have power, if an application is made under this section by that person or by the personal representative of the deceased, to vary or revoke that agreement.

(2) In exercising the powers conferred by this section the court shall have regard to all the circumstances of the case, including any order which the court proposes to make under section 2 or section 5 of this Act and any change (whether resulting from the death of the deceased or otherwise) in any of the circumstances in the light of which the agreement was made.

(3) If a maintenance agreement is varied by the court under this section the like consequences shall ensue as if the variation had been made immediately before the death of the deceased by agreement between the parties and for valuable consideration.

(4) In this section "maintenance agreement", in relation to a deceased person, means any agreement made, whether in writing or not and whether before or after the commencement of this Act, by the deceased with any person with whom he entered into a marriage, being an agreement which contained provisions governing the rights and liabilities towards one another when living separately of the parties to that marriage (whether or not the marriage has been dissolved or annulled) in respect of the making or securing of payments or the disposition or use of any property, including such rights and liabilities with respect to the maintenance or education of any child, whether or not a child of the deceased or a person who was treated by the deceased as a child of the family in relation to that marriage.

NOTE

This section enables the court in family provision proceedings to vary or revoke maintenance agreements. Compare section 36 of the Matrimonial Causes Act 1973. See p. 19, *ante*.

Availability of court's powers under this Act in applications under ss. 31 and 36 of the Matrimonial Causes Act 1973

18.—(1) Where—
(a) a person against whom a secured periodical payments order was made under the Matrimonial Causes Act 1973 has died and an application is made under section 31(6) of that Act for the variation or discharge of that order or for the revival of the operation of any provision thereof which has been suspended, or
(b) a party to a maintenance agreement within the meaning of section 34 of that Act has died, the agreement being one which provides for the continuation of payments thereunder after the death of one of the parties, and an application is made under section 36(1) of that Act for the alteration of the agreement under section 35 thereof,
the court shall have power to direct that the application made under the said section 31(6) or 36(1) shall be deemed to have been accompanied by an application for an order under section 2 of this Act.

(2) Where the court gives a direction under subsection (1) above it shall have power, in the proceedings on the application under the

said section 31(6) or 36(1), to make any order which the court would have had power to make under the provisions of this Act if the application under the said section 31(6) or 36(1), as the case may be, had been made jointly with an application for an order under the said section 2; and the court shall have power to give such consequential directions as may be necessary for enabling the court to exercise any of the powers available to the court under this Act in the case of an application for an order under section 2.

(3) Where an order made under section 15(1) of this Act is in force with respect to a party to a marriage, the court shall not give a direction under subsection (1) above with respect to any application made under the said section 31(6) or 36(1) by that party on the death of the other party.

NOTE

When an application is made under the Matrimonial Causes Act 1973 for the variation, discharge or revocation of a secured periodical payments order or a maintenance agreement after a death, this section makes available to the court the powers given by this Act, not least the power to avoid dispositions. Contrast section 37 of the Matrimonial Causes Act 1973. See p. 19, *ante*.

Miscellaneous and supplementary provisions

Effect, duration and form of orders

19.—(1) Where an order is made under section 2 of this Act then for all purposes, including the purposes of the enactments relating to capital transfer tax, the will or the law relating to intestacy, or both the will and the law relating to intestacy, as the case may be, shall have effect and be deemed to have had effect as from the deceased's death subject to the provisions of the order.

(2) Any order made under section 2 or 5 of this Act in favour of—

    (*a*) an applicant who was the former husband or former wife of the deceased, or

    (*b*) an applicant who was the husband or wife of the deceased in a case where the marriage with the deceased was the subject of a decree of judicial separation and at the date of death the decree was in force and the separation was continuing,

shall, in so far as it provides for the making of periodical payments, cease to have effect on the remarriage of the applicant, except in relation to any arrears due under the order on the date of the remarriage.

(3) A copy of every order made under this Act [other than an order made under section 15(1) of this Act] shall be sent to the principal registry of the Family Division for entry and filing, and a

memorandum of the order shall be endorsed on, or permanently annexed to, the probate or letters of administration under which the estate is being administered.

NOTE

Subsection (1) provides in effect that the order is read into the will or the intestacy rules. See p. 77, *ante*.

Subsection (2) makes periodical payment orders in favour of former spouses and judicially separated spouses terminate on their remarriage. See pp. 18, 47, *ante*.

The words in square brackets were added by s. 52 of the Administration of Justice Act 1982.

Provisions as to personal representatives

20.—(1) The provisions of this Act shall not render the personal representative of a deceased person liable for having distributed any part of the estate of the deceased, after the end of the period of six months from the date on which representation with respect to the estate of the deceased is first taken out, on the ground that he ought to have taken into account the possibility—

(*a*) that the court might permit the making of an application for an order under section 2 of this Act after the end of that period, or

(*b*) that, where an order has been made under the said section 2, the court might exercise in relation thereto the powers conferred on it by section 6 of this Act,

but this subsection shall not prejudice any power to recover, by reason of the making of an order under this Act, any part of the estate so distributed.

(2) Where the personal representative of a deceased person pays any sum directed by an order under section 5 of this Act to be paid out of the deceased's net estate, he shall not be under any liability by reason of that estate not being sufficient to make the payment, unless at the time of making the payment he has reasonable cause to believe that the estate is not sufficient.

(3) Where a deceased person entered into a contract by which he agreed to leave by his will any sum of money or other property to any person or by which he agreed that a sum of money or other property would be paid or transferred to any person out of his estate, then, if the personal representative of the deceased has reason to believe that the deceased entered into the contract with the intention of defeating an application for financial provision under this Act, he may, notwithstanding anything in that contract, postpone the payment of that sum of money or the transfer of that property until the expiration of the period of six months from the date on which representation with respect to the estate of the

deceased is first taken out or, if during that period an application is made for an order under section 2 of this Act, until the determination of the proceedings on that application.

NOTE

This section contains various provisions protecting personal representatives. See pp. 11 to 12, 65, *ante*.

Admissibility as evidence of statements made by deceased

21. In any proceedings under this Act a statement made by the deceased, whether orally or in a document or otherwise, shall be admissible under section 2 of the Civil Evidence Act 1968 as evidence of any fact stated therein in like manner as if the statement were a statement falling within section 2(1) of that Act; and any reference in that Act to a statement admissible, or given or proposed to be given, in evidence under section 2 thereof or to the admissibility or the giving in evidence of a statement by virtue of that section or to any statement falling within section 2(1) of that Act shall be construed accordingly.

NOTE

This section makes it clear that the provisions of the Civil Evidence Act 1968 rendering hearsay evidence admissible apply to statements made by a deceased person against whose estate an application is made. See p. 73, *ante*.

Jurisdiction of county courts

22. [This section was repealed by Sched. 9 of the Administration of Justice Act 1982.]

Determination of date on which representation was first taken out

23. In considering for the purposes of this Act when representation with respect to the estate of a deceased person was first taken out, a grant limited to settled land or to trust property shall be left out of account, and a grant limited to real estate or to personal estate shall be left out of account unless a grant limited to the remainder of the estate has previously been made or is made at the same time.

NOTE

This section clarifies the date when representation is taken out for the purposes of section 4, *ante*. See p. 11, *ante*.

Effect of this Act on s. 46(1)(vi) of Administration of Estates Act 1925

24. Section 46(1)(vi) of the Administration of Estates Act 1925, in so far as it provides for the devolution of property on the Crown, the Duchy of Lancaster or the Duke of Cornwall as bona vacantia, shall have effect subject to the provisions of this Act.

NOTE

This section makes it clear that the property of the deceased passing as *bona vacantia* can be made the subject of an order under the Act. See p. 55, *ante.*

Interpretation

25.—(1) In this Act:—
"beneficiary," in relation to the estate of a deceased person, means:—
(*a*) a person who under the will of the deceased or under the law relating to intestacy is beneficially interested in the estate or would be so interested if an order had not been made under this Act, and
(*b*) a person who has received any sum of money or other property which by virtue of section 8(1) or 8(2) of this Act is treated as part of the net estate of the deceased or would have received that sum or other property if an order had not been made under this Act;
"child" includes an illegitimate child and a child en ventre sa mere at the death of the deceased;
"the court" means the High Court, or where a county court has jurisdiction by virtue of section 22 of this Act, a county court;
["former wife" or "former husband" means a person whose marriage with the deceased was during the lifetime of the deceased either—
(*a*) dissolved or annulled by a decree of divorce or a decree of nullity of marriage granted under the law of any part of the British Islands, or
(*b*) dissolved or annulled in any country or territory outside the British Islands by a divorce or annulment which is entitled to be recognised as valid by the law of England and Wales;]
"net estate," in relation to a deceased person, means:—
(*a*) all property of which the deceased had power to dispose by his will (otherwise than by virtue of a

special power of appointment) less the amount of his funeral, testamentary and administration expenses, debts and liabilities, including any capital transfer tax payable out of his estate on his death;

(*b*) any property in respect of which the deceased held a general power of appointment (not being a power exercisable by will) which has not been exercised;

(*c*) any sum of money or other property which is treated for the purposes of this Act as part of the net estate of the deceased by virtue of section 8(1) or (2) of this Act;

(*d*) any property which is treated for the purposes of this Act as part of the net estate of the deceased by virtue of an order made under section 9 of the Act;

(*e*) any sum of money or other property which is, by reason of a disposition or contract made by the deceased, ordered under section 10 or 11 of this Act to be provided for the purpose of the making of financial provision under this Act;

"property" includes any chose in action;

"reasonable financial provision" has the meaning assigned to it by section 1 of this Act;

"valuable consideration" does not include marriage or a promise of marriage;

"will" includes codicil.

(2) For the purposes of paragraph (*a*) of the definition of "net estate" in subsection (1) above a person who is not of full age and capacity shall be treated as having power to dispose by a will of all property of which he would have had power to dispose by will if he had been of full age and capacity.

(3) Any reference in this Act to provision out of the net estate of a deceased person includes a reference to provision extending to the whole of that estate.

(4) For the purposes of this Act any reference to a wife or husband shall be treated as including a reference to a person who in good faith entered into a void marriage with the deceased unless either:—

(*a*) the marriage of the deceased and that person was dissolved or annulled during the lifetime of the deceased and the dissolution or annulment is recognised by the law of England and Wales, or

(*b*) that person has during the lifetime of the deceased entered into a later marriage.

(5) Any reference in this Act to remarriage or to a person who has remarried includes a reference to a marriage which is by law void or voidable or to a person who has entered into such a marriage, as the case may be, and a marriage shall be treated for the purposes of this Act as a remarriage, in relation to any party thereto, notwithstanding that the previous marriage of that party was void or voidable.

(6) Any reference in this Act to an order or decree made under the Matrimonial Causes Act 1973 or under any section of that Act shall be construed as including a reference to an order or decree which is deemed to have been made under that Act or under that section thereof, as the case may be.

(7) Any reference in this Act to any enactment is a reference to that enactment as amended by or under any subsequent enactment.

NOTE

This is the definition section. All of it is important, but note especially the definitions of "beneficiary," "child," "net estate," and "valuable consideration"; also the explanations of references to a wife or husband in subsection (4), and to remarriage in subsection (5).

In section 25(1) the definition of "former wife" and "former husband" was substituted by s. 25 of the Matrimonial and Family Proceedings Act 1984.

Consequential amendments, repeals and transitional provisions

26.—(1) Section 36 of the Matrimonial Causes Act 1973 (which provides for the alteration of maintenance agreements by the High Court or a county court after the death of one of the parties) shall have effect subject to the following amendments (being amendments consequential on this Act), that is to say—

(a) in subsection (3) for the words "section 7 of the Family Provision Act 1966" there shall be substituted the words "section 22 of the Inheritance (Provision for Family and Dependants) Act 1975," for the words from "the Inheritance (Family Provision) Act" to "net estate" there shall be substituted the words "that Act if the value of the property mentioned in that section" and for the words "section 26 of the Matrimonial Causes Act 1965 (application for maintenance out of deceased's estate by former spouse)" there shall be substituted the words "section 2 of that Act";

(b) in subsection (7) for the words from "section 7" to "subsection (5)" there shall be substituted the words "section 22 of the Inheritance (Provision for Family and Dependants) Act 1975 (which enables rules of court to provide for the transfer from a county court to the High Court or from the High Court to a county court of proceedings for an order under section 2 of that Act) and paragraphs (*a*) and (*b*) of subsection (4)" and for the words "any such proceedings as are referred to in subsection (1) of that section" there shall be substituted the words "proceedings for an order under section 2 of that Act."

(2) Subject to the provisions of this section, the enactments specified in the Schedule to this Act are hereby repealed to the extent specified in the third column of the Schedule; and in paragraph 5(2) of Schedule 2 to the Matrimonial Causes Act 1973 for the words "that Act" there shall be substituted the words "the Matrimonial Causes Act 1965."

(3) The repeal of the said enactments shall not affect their operation in relation to any application made thereunder (whether before or after the commencement of this Act) with reference to the death of any person who died before the commencement of this Act.

(4) Without prejudice to the provisions of section 38 of the Interpretation Act 1889 (which relates to the effect of repeals) nothing in any repeal made by this Act shall affect any order made or direction given under any enactment repealed by this Act, and, subject to the provisions of this Act, every such order or direction (other than an order made under section 4A of the Inheritance Family Provision Act 1938 or section 28A of the Matrimonial Causes Act 1965) shall, if it is in force at the commencement of this Act or is made by virtue of subsection (3) above, continue in force as if it had been made under section 2(1)(*a*) of this Act, and for the purposes of section 6(7) of this Act the court in exercising its powers under that section in relation to an order continued in force by this subsection shall be required to have regard to any change in any of the circumstances to which the court would have been required to have regard when making that order if the order had been made with reference to the death of any person who died after the commencement of this Act.

NOTE

Note especially subsection (3), which preserves the 1938 and the 1965 Acts for deaths before the commencement of the new Act, and subsection (4), which makes clear that the power of variation in section 6 applies to orders made under the old Acts. See p. 51, *ante*.

Short title, commencement and extent

27.—(1) This Act may be cited as the Inheritance (Provision for Family and Dependants) Act 1975.

(2) This Act does not extend to Scotland or Northern Ireland.

(3) This Act shall come into force on 1st April 1976.

SCHEDULE

ENACTMENTS REPEALED

Chapter	Short Title	Extent of Repeal
1938 c.72	The Inheritance (Family Provision) Act 1938.	The whole Act.
1952 c. 64.	The Intestates' Estates Act 1952.	Section 7 and Schedule 3.
1965 c. 72.	The Matrimonial Causes Act 1965.	Sections 26 to 26A and section 25 (4) and (4) as applied by section 28 (2).
1966 c. 35.	The Family Provision Act 1966.	The whole Act, except section 1 and sub-sections (1) and (3) of section 10.
1969 c. 46.	The Family Law Reform Act 1969.	Sections 5 (1) and 18.
1970 c. 31.	The Administration of Justice Act 1970.	In Schedule 2, paragraph 16.
1970 c. 33.	The Law Reform (Miscellaneous Provisions) Act 1970.	Section 6.
1970 c. 45.	The Matrimonial Proceedings and Property Act 1970.	Section 36.
1971 c. 23.	The Courts Act 1971.	Section 45 (1) (a).
1973 c. 18.	The Matrimonial Causes Act 1973.	In section 50, in subsection (1) (a) the words from "and sections 26" to the end of the paragraph, in subsection (1) (d) the words "or sections 26 to 28A of the Matrimonial Causes Act 1965" and in subsection (2) (a) the words "or under section 26 or 27 of the Matrimonial Causes Act 1965." In Schedule 2, paragraph 5 (1) and in paragraph 12 the words "(a) sections 26 to 28A of the Matrimonial Causes Act 1965."
1975 c. 7.	The Finance Act 1975.	In Schedule 12, paragraph 6.

Appendix 2

Order 99

Inheritance (Provision for Family and Dependants) Act 1975

Interpretation (O. 99, r. 1)

1. In this Order "the Act" means the Inheritance (Provision for Family and Dependants) Act 1975 and a section referred to by number means the section so numbered in that Act.

Assignment to Chancery or Family Division (O. 99, r. 2)

2. Proceedings in the High Court under the Act may be assigned to the Chancery Division or to the Family Division.

Application for financial provision (O. 99, r. 3)

3.—(1) Any originating summons by which an application under section 1 is made may be issued out of Chancery Chambers, the principal registry of the Family Division or any district registry.

(2) The summons shall be in Form No. 10 in Appendix A.

(3) There shall be lodged with the Court an affidavit by the applicant in support of the summons, exhibiting an official copy of the grant of representation to the deceased's estate and of every testamentary document admitted to proof, and a copy of the affidavit shall be served on every defendant with the summons.

Para. (2) substituted by R.S.C. (Writ and Appearance) 1979 (S.I. 1979 No. 1716).

Powers of Court as to parties (O. 99, r. 4)

4.—(1) Without prejudice to its powers under Order 15, the Court may at any stage of proceedings under the Act direct that any person be added as a party to the proceedings or that notice of the proceedings be served on any person.

(2) Order 15, rule 13, shall apply to proceedings under the Act as it applies to the proceedings mentioned in paragraph (1) of that rule.

Affidavit in answer (O. 99, r. 5)

5.—(1) A defendant to an application under section 1 who is a personal representative of the deceased shall and any other defendant may, within 21 days after service of the summons on him, inclusive of the day of service, lodge with the Court an affidavit in answer to the application.

(2) The affidavit lodged by a personal representative pursuant to paragraph (1) shall state to the best of the deponent's ability—

(*a*) full particulars of the value of the deceased's net estate, as defined by section 25(1);

(*b*) the person or classes of persons beneficially interested in the estate, giving the names and (in the case of those who are not already parties) the addresses of all living beneficiaries, and the value of their interests so far as ascertained;

(*c*) if such be the case, that any living beneficiary (naming him) is a minor or a patient within the meaning of Order 80, rule 1; and

(*d*) any facts known to the deponent which might affect the exercise of the Court's powers under the Act.

(3) Every defendant who lodges an affidavit shall at the same time serve a copy on the plaintiff and on every other defendant who is not represented by the same solicitor.

Separate representation (O. 99, r. 6)

6. Where an application under section 1 is made jointly by two or more applicants and the originating summons is accordingly issued by one solicitor on behalf of all of them, they may, if they have conflicting interests, appear on any hearing of the summons by separate solicitors or counsel or in person, and where at any stage of the proceedings it appears to the Court that one of the applicants is not but ought to be separately represented, the Court may adjourn the proceedings until he is.

Endorsement of memorandum on grant (O. 99, r. 7)

7. On the hearing of an application under section 1 the personal representative shall produce to the Court the grant of representation to the deceased's estate and, if an order is made under the Act, the grant shall remain in the custody of the Court until a memorandum of the order has been endorsed on or permanently annexed to the grant in accordance with section 19(3).

Disposal of proceedings in chambers (O. 99, r. 8)

8. Any proceedings under the Act may, if the Court so directs, be disposed of in chambers and Order 32, rule 14(1) shall apply in relation to proceedings in the Family Division as if for the words the Masters of the Chancery Division there were substituted the words "A registrar of the Family Division shall."

Amended by R.S.C. (Amendment No. 2) 1982 (S.I. 1982 No. 1111).

Subsequent applications in proceedings under section 1 (O. 99, r. 9)

9. Where an order has been made on an application under section 1, any subsequent application under the Act, whether made by a party to the proceedings or by any other person, shall be made by summons in those proceedings.

Drawing up and service of orders (O. 99, r. 10)

10. The provisions of the Matrimonial Causes Rules relating to the drawing up and service of orders shall apply to proceedings in the Family Division under this Order as if they were proceedings under those Rules.

Transfer to county court (O. 99, r. 11)

11.—(1) Where an application to which section 22(1) relates is within the jurisdiction of a county court, the Court may, if the parties consent or it appears to the Court to be desirable, order the transfer of the application to such county court as appears to the Court to be most convenient to the parties.

(2) An order under paragraph (1) may be made by the Court of its own motion or on the application of any party, but before making an order of its own motion otherwise than by consent the Court shall give the parties an opportunity of being heard on the question of transfer and for that purpose the master or registrar may give the parties notice of a date, time and place at which the question will be considered.

Substituted by R.S.C. (Amendment) 1976 (S.I. 1976 No. 337).

See also:
Practice Note (Inheritance: Family Provision)[1976] 1 W.L.R.418.
Practice Direction (Family Provision: Application)[1978] 1 W.L.R.585.
Practice Direction (Family Provision: Endorsement of Order)[1979] 1 W.L.R.1.

Appendix 3

Order 48

FAMILY PROVISION

Interpretation

1. In this Order—

"the Act of 1973" means the Matrimonial Causes Act 1973;

"the Act of 1975" means the Inheritance (Provision for Family and Dependants) Act 1975;

"the deceased" means, in the case of an application under section 36 of the Act of 1973 the deceased party to the agreement to which the application relates and, in the case of an application under section 1 of the Act of 1975, the person to whose estate the application relates.

Mode of application

2.—(1) An application to a county court under section 1 of the Act of 1975 for provision to be made out of the estate of a deceased person shall be made by originating application stating—

(*a*) the name of the deceased, the date of his death and his country of domicile that date;

(*b*) the relationship of the applicant to the deceased or other qualification of the applicant for making the application;

(*c*) the date on which representation with respect to the deceased's estate was first taken out and the names and addresses of the personal representatives;

(*d*) that to the best of the applicant's knowledge and belief the value of the deceased's net estate does not exceed the sum for the time being fixed under section 22(1) of the Act of 1975;

(*e*) whether the disposition of the deceased's estate effected by his will or the law relating to intestacy was such as to make any provision for the applicant and, if it was, the nature of the provision;

(*f*) to the best of the applicant's knowledge and belief, the persons or classes of persons interested in the deceased's estate and the nature of their interests;

(*g*) particulars of the applicant's present and foreseeable financial resources and financial needs and any other information which he desires to place before the court on the matters to which the court is required to have regard under section 3 of the Act of 1975;

(*h*) where appropriate, a request for the court's permission to make the application notwithstanding that the period of six months has expired from the date on which representation in regard to the estate of the deceased was first taken out, and the grounds of the request; and

(*i*) the nature of the provision applied for.

(2) An application to a county court under section 36 of the Act of 1973 for the alteration of a maintenance agreement after the death of one of the parties shall be made by originating application giving the information which would be required to be stated in a supporting affidavit if the application were made to the High Court and also, in the case of an application by the surviving party to the agreement, stating that to the best of the applicant's knowledge and belief the value of the deceased's net estate does not exceed the sum for the time being fixed under section 22(1) of the Act of 1975.

Filing of application

3.—(1) An application to which rule 2(1) or (2) relates shall be filed—

(*a*) in the court for the district in which the deceased resided at the date of his death, or

(*b*) if the deceased did not then reside in England or Wales, in the court for the district in which the respondent or one of the respondents resides or carried on business or the estate or part of the estate is situate, or

(*c*) if neither of the foregoing sub-paragraphs is applicable, in the court for the district in which the applicant resides or carries on business.

(2) The applicant shall file with his originating application—

(*a*) an official copy of the grant of representation to the deceased's estate and of every testamentary document admitted to proof, and

(*b*) in the case of an application under section 36 of the Act of 1973, a copy of the agreement to which the application relates.

(3) Unless the court otherwise directs, the return day of the originating application shall be a day fixed for the pre-trial review of the proceedings.

Parties

4.—(1) Without prejudice to its powers under Orders 5 and 15, the court may, at any stage of the proceedings, direct that any person be added as a party to the proceedings or that notice of the proceedings be served on any person.

(2) Order 5, rule 6, shall apply to an application under section 1 of the Act of 1975 or section 36 of the Act of 1973 as it applies to the proceedings mentioned in that rule.

Answer

5. Every respondent shall, within 21 days after service of the originating application on him, file an answer, which, if the respondent is a personal representative, shall state to the best of his ability—

(*a*) full particulars of the value of the deceased's net estate, as defined by section 25(1) of the Act of 1975;

(*b*) the persons or classes of persons beneficially interested in the estate, giving the names and (in the case of those who are not already parties) the addresses of all living beneficiaries, and the value of their interests so far as ascertained;

(*c*) if such be the case, that any living beneficiary (naming him) is a minor or a mental patient; and

(*d*) in the case of an application under section 1 of the Act of 1975, any facts known to the personal representative which might affect exercise of the court's powers under that Act.

Subsequent application

6. Where an order has been made on an application under section 1 of the Act of 1975, any subsequent application, whether made by a party to the proceedings or by any other person, shall be made in those proceedings in accordance with Order 13, rule 1.

Hearing

7. Any application under section 1 of the Act of 1975 or section 36 of the Act of 1973 may be heard and determined by the registrar and may, if the court thinks fit, be dealt with in chambers.

Endorsement of memorandum on grant

8. On the hearing of an application under section 1 of the Act of 1975, the personal representative shall produce to the court the grant of representation to the deceased's estate and, if an order is made under the Act, the proper officer shall send a sealed copy thereof, together with the grant of representation, to the principal registry of the Family Division for a memorandum of the order to be endorsed on, or permanently annexed to, the grant in accordance with section 19(3) of the Act of 1975.

Transfer to High Court

9.—(1) The court in which an application under section 36 of the Act of 1973 or section 1 of the Act of 1975 is pending may order the transfer of the application to the High Court where the transfer appears to the court to be desirable.

(2) In considering whether an application should be transferred under paragraph (1) from a county court to the High Court, the court shall have regard to all relevant considerations, including the nature and value of the property involved, the relative expense of proceeding in the High Court and the county court and the limit for the time being of the jurisdiction of county courts under section 22 of the Act of 1975.

(3) Any order of transfer shall state whether it is desired that the proceedings be assigned to the Chancery Division or to the Family Division of the High Court.

N. 423
Originating Application for Reasonable Financial Provision under Section 1 of Inheritance (Provision for Family and Dependants) Act 1975

Order 48, rule 2(1)

[General Title—Form N 200]

1. I   of
apply to the Court for an order under section 1 of the Inheritance (Provision for Family and Dependants) Act 1975 for reasonable financial provision to be made for me out of the estate of
who died on the   day of   19   being
domiciled in England and Wales and resident at   .

2. I am the wife [*or* husband] of the deceased [*or state in what other way the applicant claims to be entitled to make the application*].

3. A grant of probate [*or* letters of administration] in regard to the estate of the deceased was first taken out on the   day

of   19
and the personal representative[s] is [are]   of
                    [and   of   ].
4. To the best of my knowledge and belief the value of the deceased's net estate does not exceed £30,000.

5. The disposition of the deceased's estate effected by his will [*or* by the law relating to intestacy] [*or* by the combination of his will and the law relating to intestacy] was such as to make no provision for me [*or* to make the following provision for me, namely   ].

6. To the best of my knowledge and belief the persons or classes of persons interested in the estate and the nature of their interests are as follows:—

7. The following are particulars of my present and foreseeable financial resources and financial needs [*give details and add any other information which the applicant desires to place before the Court on the matters to which the Court is required to have regard under section 3 of the Act*].

8. [*Insert where appropriate*] I request the Court's permission to make this application notwithstanding that the period of six months has expired from the date on which representation in regard to the estate of the deceased was first taken out, and the grounds of my request are as follows:—

9. I ask for reasonable financial provision to be made for me out of the deceased's estate by way of an order for [*state nature of order applied for*].

10. The names and addresses of the respondents on whom this application is intended to be served are—

11. My address for service is:—

Dated this   day of   19   .

APPLICANT

TO THE RESPONDENT

Within 21 days after service of this application on you, inclusive of the day of service, you must file in the court office an answer, together with a copy for every other party to the proceedings, containing a statement of your case and, if you are a personal representative of the deceased:—

(a) full particulars of the value of the deceased's net estate;

(b) the persons or classes of persons beneficially interested in the estate (including the names and addresses of all living beneficiaries and whether any of them is a minor or a mental patient); and

(c) any facts known to you which might affect the exercise of the Court's powers under the Act.

N. 424
Originating Application for Alteration of Maintenance Agreement

Order 48, rule 2(2)

[General Title—Form N. 200]

1. I [We]   of   apply to the Court for an order under section 35 of the Matrimonial Causes Act 1973 that the agreement made on the   day of   19 between [me and]   who died on the   day of   19   [and the respondent] should be altered so as to make different [*or* contain] financial arrangements.

2. A grant of probate [*or* letters of administration] in regard to the estate of the deceased was first taken out on the   day of   19 and the personal representative[s] is [are]   of   [and]   of [or and I am [we are] the personal representative[s]]

3. Immediately before his death the deceased was domiciled in England and Wales.

4. The deceased and I [*or* the Respondent] (formerly [*name and status*] were married at   on the   day of   19   .

5. There is [are] [no [*or state number*] child[ren] of the family [namely] [*state the name of each child and his date of birth or, if it be the case, that he is over 18*]. The said [*name of each child under 18*] reside(s) with [*name and address of person with whom each child resides*].

6. [The agreement also makes financial arrangements for the following child[ren] namely [*state the name of each child and his date of birth or, if it be the case, that he is over 18*]].

7. [*Where any child mentioned in paragraph 5 or 6 has died since the agreement was made*]. The said [*state name*] died on the   day of   19   .

8. To the best of my knowledge and belief—

(a) the value of the deceased's net estate does not exceed £30,000;

(b) the persons or classes of persons beneficially interested in the estate and the nature of their interests are as follows:—

or where the applicant[s] is a [are] personal representative[s]
(a) The value of the deceased's net estate is £
(b) The persons or classes of persons beneficially interested in the estate are [*state names and addresses of all known beneficiaries and whether any of them is under 18 or a mental patient*] and the value of their interests so far ascertained is
9. There have been no previous proceedings in any court with reference to the agreement or to the marriage [or to any child[ren] of the family [or to the other child[ren] for whom the agreement makes financial arrangements]] [except [*state the nature of the proceedings and the date and effect of any decree or order*]]
10. There have been no proceedings in any court against the deceased's estate under the Inheritance (Provision for Family and Dependants) Act 1975 or section 26 of the Matrimonial Causes Act 1965 [except [*state the nature of the proceedings and the date and effect of any decree or order*]]
11. The following are particulars of my means:—

or where the applicant[s] is a [are] personal representative[s]:—
To the best of my [our] knowledge and belief the respondent's means are as follows:—
12. I [We] ask the following alteration to be made in the agreement for the following reasons:—
13. [*Insert where appropriate*] I [We] request the Court's permission to make this application notwithstanding that the period of six months from the date on which representation in regard to the estate of the deceased was first taken out has expired, and the grounds of my [our] request are as follows:—
14. The names and addresses of the respondents on whom this application is intended to be served are:—
15. My [Our] address for service is:-

Dated this   day of   19   .

APPLICANT[S]

[Conclusion as in Form N. 423 omitting paragraph (c)]

Appendix 4

1. Draft Originating Summons

IN THE HIGH COURT OF JUSTICE   1985 No.
  DIVISION
  [DISTRICT REGISTRY]

IN THE MATTER of the Estate of   Deceased

BETWEEN:

               Plaintiff

       –and–

             Defendant(s)

LET   of
attend before [Master —— at Chancery Chambers, Room No.
——, Royal Courts of Justice, Strand, London WC2A 2LL.] [Mr
Registrar —— in Chambers, at the Divorce Registry, Somerset
House, London WC2R 1LP] [the District Registrar at] [——] [on
—— day the —— day of —— at —— o'clock] [on a day to be fixed]
on the hearing of an application by the Plaintiff —— for an order:–

[1. That she may have permission to make an application under the
Inheritance (Provision for Family and Dependants) Act 1975
notwithstanding that a period of six months from the date upon
which representation in regard to the estate of the above named
Deceased was first taken out has ended.]

2. That she may be granted reasonable financial provision out of the
estate of the said deceased.

3. That provision may be made for the costs of this application.

This application is made under the Inheritance (Provision for
Family and Dependants) Act 1975

AND LET the Defendant within 14 days after service of this
Summons on him, counting the day of service, return the
accompanying Acknowledgment of Service to the appropriate
Court Office.

DATED, etc. ....

NOTE:—This Summons may not be served less than 12 calendar months beginning with the above date unless renewed by order of the Court.

THIS SUMMONS was taken out by . . . etc.

NOTE:—If a defendant does not attend personally or by his counsel or solicitor at the time and place above mentioned such order will be made as the court may think just and expedient.

A defendant who is a personal representative must, within 21 days after service of this Summons on him, counting the day of service, lodge with the court an affidavit in answer, stating the particulars required by Order 99, rule 5, of the Rules of the Supreme Court.

IMPORTANT

Directions for acknowledgment of service are given with the accompanying form.

2 Draft Affidavit by Spouse

IN THE HIGH COURT OF JUSTICE   1985 T.No.
FAMILY DIVISION

IN THE MATTER of the Estate of Job Trotter deceased

BETWEEN:

NANCY TROTTER

Plaintiff

–and–

(1) BENJAMIN HORATIO PERKER
(2) JOHN EDWARD STIGGINS
(3) DARREN PETER STIGGINS
(4) XANTHE JANE STIGGINS
(5) JOHN SAMUEL WELLER
(6) ROSEMARY LOUISE WELLER

Defendants

I, NANCY TROTTER, old age pensioner, of "Stubbins House" Eatanswill, in the County of Suffolk, make oath and say as follows:

1. I am the Plaintiff in these proceedings. I am 82 years of age. My late husband Job Trotter, the above named deceased, died on the

20th December 1984, and his Will was proved by the First Defendant on the 3rd March 1985.

2. I married the deceased on 6th April 1925. There is now produced and shown to be marked "NT 1" an official copy of my marriage certificate. As far as I am concerned our marriage was a very happy one, and I have no reason to suppose that the deceased was anything other than happy in our marriage.

3. The deceased made his Will on 11th June 1978, and appointed the Defendant his sole executor. By his Will he gave me the right to remain in the matrimonial home until my own death, and gave me the residue of his estate absolutely. The matrimonial home was to be sold when I ceased to reside there, and the proceeds of its sale were to be then divided between the deceased's grandchildren living at his death and attaining the age of 21 years in equal shares. There is now produced and shown to me together marked "NT 2" an official copy of the grant of Probate and of the Will of the deceased.

4. When the Will was made in 1978 my health was quite good. However, I am now totally blind and am in need of assistance in my everyday life. I have therefore moved to the Suffolk County Council Residential Home called "Stubbins House" at Eatanswill. Because I have moved out of the former matrimonial home the First Defendant has asked me for my written authority to sell it, which I have given. The house has now been sold and the net proceeds of its sale amount to £32,765.00.

5. The effect of the Will is that, once the former matrimonial home has been sold, the net proceeds thereof fall to be divided between the grandchildren of the deceased, and I receive nothing from such net proceeds. The residue under the Will consists of approximately £300 in cash, and a few personal chattels of no significant monetary value. I therefore consider and am advised that the Will does not make sufficient provision for me. The surviving grandchildren who take under the Will are the Second to Sixth Defendants herein. Two of them, namely the Fifth and Sixth Defendants John Samuel Weller and Rosemary Louise Weller, are not yet of full age.

6. The charges made by the County Council for accommodation at "Stubbins House" are on a sliding scale proportionate to the resident's income and capital. The sliding scale is identical with that used by the Department of Health and Social Security for assessing resources for the purposes of supplementary benefit. By virtue of Regulation 6(2) of the Supplementary Benefit (Resources) Regulations of 1981, as amended by the Supplementary Benefit (Uprating) Regulations 1983, capital resources not exceeding £3,000 are disregarded in calculating the weekly sums payable by residents. It

has therefore been agreed between myself, the Second, Third and Fourth Defendants, and the guardian *ad litem* of the Fifth and Sixth Defendants, that these proceedings will be compromised on terms that I receive a total of £3,000 from the estate of the deceased, and nothing more. I understand that the Court must approve this compromise because the Fifth and Sixth Defendants are not all of full age.

7. My sole income is the ordinary old age pension, at present £35.80 a week. The County Council take all of this except £4 a week, under the sliding scale. I have no other income and no savings.

8. In the circumstances as explained above, I respectfully ask the Court to approve the compromise which has been reached in these proceedings, and to make the appropriate order.

SWORN etc.

3. Draft Affidavit by Guardian Ad Litem

[*Heading as precedent 2, above*]

I, NATHANIEL HARRY WINKLE, of 12 The Pastures, Eatanswill in the County of Suffolk, make oath and say as follows:

1. I am an old friend of the Weller family, being one of the godparents of the Sixth Defendant herein. As such I was asked to be, consented to be, and now am, the guardian *ad litem* of the Fifth and Sixth Defendants.

2. The compromise which has been proposed in these proceedings has always seemed to me to be eminently sensible. I have through my solicitors instructed Counsel to advise on it, and he has advised to the same effect. There are now produced and shown together marked "NHW" my solicitor's Instructions to Counsel and Counsel's Opinion.

3. I believe that the proposed compromise is in the best interests of the Fifth and Sixth Defendants, and I respectfully request that it be approved.

SWORN etc.

4. Draft Order

[*Heading as precedent 2, above*]

UPON THE APPLICATION of the Plaintiff by Originating Summons dated

AND UPON HEARING the solicitors for the Plaintiff and the First Defendant respectively and Counsel for the Fifth and Sixth Defendants

AND UPON READING the said Originating Summons and the affidavits filed herein respectively by the Plaintiff on —— the First Defendant on —— and the guardian *ad litem* of the Fifth and Sixth Defendants on ——
[In Chancery Division; UPON READING the documents recorded in the Court file as having been read]

AND the Plaintiff and the First Defendant by their respective solicitors and the Second, Third and Fourth Defendants by letters from their solicitors stating that they have agreed to the terms set forth in the Schedule hereto and consenting to this order

AND THE REGISTRAR being satisfied that the said terms are for the benefit of the minor parties hereto being the Fifth Defendant John Samuel Weller and the Sixth Defendant Rosemary Louise Weller

HEREBY APPROVES the said terms on behalf of the said minors

AND IT IS ORDERED the costs of the Plaintiff and the Second to Sixth Defendants of and incidental to the said application be taxed on the common fund basis (if such costs are not agreed between the parties hereto)

AND IT IS ORDERED the costs of the Plaintiff and the Fifth and Sixth Defendants be taxed in accordance with the provisions of the Second Schedule to the Legal Aid Act 1974 should taxation be required by the Law Society but not otherwise

AND IT IS ORDERED that all further proceedings in this application be stayed except for the purpose of carrying the said terms into effect

AND for that purpose the parties are to be at liberty to apply.

THE SCHEDULE

1. The Plaintiff shall receive the sum of £2,700 out of the proceeds of sale of the dwellinghouse of the above named deceased now held

upon deposit by the First Defendant in an account at the Fleet and Marshalsea Building Society.

2. Subject to the said payment and to the provision for costs, charges and disbursements hereinafter contained the estate of the said deceased shall be administered and distributed in accordance with his Will as the same was proved by the First Defendant at the Ipswich Probate Registry on ——

3. The costs of the First Defendant as trustee of and incidental to the said application and his charges and disbursements as executor of the Will of the said deceased shall be paid out of the said proceeds of sale.

4. The costs of the Second to Sixth Defendants of and incidental to this application if not agreed shall be taxed on the common fund basis (the solicitors for the Fifth and Sixth Defendants being the minor Defendants waiving any further solicitor and own client costs) and such costs shall be paid out of the said proceeds of sale.

5. Draft Affidavit by Adult Child

IN THE HIGH COURT OF JUSTICE   1985 S.No.
CHANCERY DIVISION

IN THE MATTER OF Annabel Jarndyce deceased

BETWEEN:

ANNE MARY SKIMPOLE

Plaintiff

–and–

(1) FREDERICK CHARLES JARNDYCE
(2) GEORGE VHOLES and
(3) THOMAS WOODCOURT

Defendants

I, ANNE MARY SKIMPOLE, of 12 Gradgrind Road, Coketown, Yorkshire, housewife and part time secretary, make oath and say as follows:

1. I am the above named Plaintiff. I make this affidavit from my own knowledge, except where the contrary appears, and my means of knowledge sufficiently appear herein.

2. I am the only daughter of the above named Annabel Jarndyce, to whom I will hereinafter refer as "the Deceased." The First

Defendant is my stepfather, the widower of the Deceased, who is one of her executors. The Second Defendant is another executor; he was the Deceased's solicitor. The Third Defendant is my brother, the only son of the Deceased, who is the third and only other executor.

3. I am now 40 years of age, having been born on the 1st June 1945, and the Third Defendant is 42, having been born on 3rd March 1943. Our father, the first husband of the Deceased, was an officer in the Royal Air Force, who was killed in a flying accident when I was 5 years old. About 3 years later, on 7th September 1953, the Deceased married the First Defendant, who was then, and as he has remained throughout his working life, a research scientist with International Pharmaceuticals Limited of Coketown.

4. It is only right and proper for me to say that the First Defendant was a good stepfather to the Third Defendant and myself, and a good husband to the Deceased. The Deceased worked part time as a teacher after my father died, and she continued with her part time job for some years after she had married the First Defendant. However, she did not increase the number of hours she worked, in fact she rather decreased them and the First Defendant's salary was the major source of the family income.

5. I qualified as a secretary when I was 19, and I married my present husband when I was 23. During the four years between I worked full time, sometimes in Coketown and sometimes in London. When I was working in Coketown I lived at home and paid the Deceased for my board and lodging.

6. When I married the Deceased gave my husband and myself a cheque for £5,000 as a wedding present. She also gave the First Defendant £5,000 when he married, about ten years ago. I have two children: Sally who is 14 and John who is 10.

7. Five years ago the First Defendant retired. In the year or two before his retirement he and the Deceased had built for them a large modern bungalow at Ghylldale, a village in the Yorkshire Dales, and when the First Defendant retired they went up there to live.

8. On 17th October 1984 my mother died, suddenly and unexpectedly. By her Will dated 27th July 1981 she gave me 5 pieces of jewellery, in effect all her jewellery of any financial or sentimental value. She gave my brother, the First Defendant, a pair of silver candlesticks which had been in her mother's family for some generations, and also a valuable antique chest. She gave pecuniary legacies of £500 each to two old friends of hers. All the residue of her property she gave to the Third Defendant absolutely. That

residue is worth about £50,000 net. There are now produced and shown to me together marked "AMS 1" official copies of my mother's Will and the grant of Probate thereof. As I have already mentioned, the executors were the Defendants.

9. I believe from remarks made by the First and Third Defendants both before and after the death of the Deceased that she and the First Defendant were the joint owners of the bungalow, and that the Deceased's interest passed to the First Defendant automatically on her death, but the Defendants have not yet formally confirmed this.

10. My financial circumstances have now become very bad. For some time before the death of the Deceased my husband's business had been in financial difficulties, and shortly after her death it failed completely. The Bank appointed a Receiver, who sold all the assets of the business, and also our home, over which the Bank had a charge. We were left virtually penniless. My husband could not, and still cannot, find other employment. I managed to find part time work as a secretary. Fortunately my husband's family have been kind and generous and have managed, at considerable financial sacrifice to themselves, to make us an interest free loan. This has been enough, with the remains of the proceeds of sale of our former home, for us to buy a small house to live in. My income, my husband's unemployment benefit, and child benefit for our two children, are enough for us to live on, provided that we give up everything except necessities. However, our children's education will be gravely affected. Our daughter Sally is at Coketown Girls Grammar School, and is due to take her "O levels' in less than two years. Coketown Girls Grammar School was a direct grant school, but is now independent, so there are fees to pay; those for Sally were nearly £1,500 last year. Our son John is due to start at King Edward's Grammar School, Coketown next year. The fees there are at least as high as those at the Girls Grammar School.

11. I will now set out our income and expenditure, as follows:

Rates (including water rates)	£33.33 per calendar month (£400 a year)
Food	£110 per calendar month
Miscellaneous household expenses	£15 per calendar month
Clothing	£20 per calendar month
Motor expenses	£50 per calendar month
Holidays	£42 per month (£500 a year approx.)
Gas	£30 per calendar month (£360 a year)

Electricity	£30 per calendar month
	(£360 a year)
Miscellaneous	£20 per calendar month,
	approximately)
House and contents insurance	£ 6 per calendar month
Life Assurances	£12 per calendar month

368.33

Our incomes consists of the following:

Unemployment Benefit	£123.28 per calendar month
	(28.45 a week)
Child Benefit	£ 59.37 per calendar month
My earnings	£185.68 per calendar month,
	after tax and other
	deductions

My husband's unemployment benefit will cease in about 2 months, when he has been unemployed for a year. I hope to make up the shortfall in our income by increasing my hours of work, but may not be able to do so.

It will be seen that our income is no more than enough for bare necessities, and that there is nothing to spare for school fees.

12. In contrast to the comparative poverty of myself and my family, the First Defendant is in a very comfortable financial position. He is the sole owner of his bungalow, which I would estimate, from my knowledge of Ghylldale, to be worth at least £60,000. He has a pension from International Pharmaceuticals; as a result of conversations with him, I believe the pension is index linked, and amounts to at least £10,000 a year at present. He also has the state retirement pension. Lastly, he has savings of his own, including the lump sum he received on his retirement from International Pharmaceuticals. I conjecture, on my general knowledge as to the amount of lump sum on retirement that a person in his position in a large public company would receive, that his savings may be as much as £50,000.

13. I therefore submit that the Deceased's Will does not make reasonable financial provision for me, and respectfully request this Honourable Court to make an order in my favour under the Inheritance (Provision for Family and Dependants) Act 1975.

SWORN etc.

6. Draft Affidavit By Independent Executor

[*Heading as precedent 5, above*]

I, GEORGE VHOLES, a Solicitor of the Supreme Court practising as a partner in the firm of Vholes Son & Buckle at 32 Silk Street, Coketown, Yorkshire make oath and say as follows:

1. I am the Second Defendant herein, and am one of the three executors of the above named Annabel Jarndyce, deceased, the other two executors being the First and Third Defendants. Except where the contrary appears, I make this affidavit as such executor, from my own knowledge acquired while acting as executor and also from my own knowledge acquired while acting as solicitor for the deceased and the First Defendant before the death of the deceased.

2. The estate of the deceased was sworn for probate at a value of £52,745 gross and £51,222 net. It consisted of the following assets:

5,000 £1 ordinary shares in International Pharmaceuticals Ltd.	£15,760
3,000 £1 ordinary shares in Capital & Counties Bank Ltd.	£12,012
2,000 £1 ordinary shares in Shropshire Land Investments Ltd.	£3,845
10,115 Multinvest 10p income units	£3,321
Dalesman Building Society special account	£12,762
Deposit account at Northern Bank Ltd., Ghylldale	£3,770
Current account at Northern Bank Ltd., Ghylldale	£1,275

3. The deceased was immediately before her death the joint owner at law and in equity with the First Defendant of the bungalow "Scarr View" Ghylldale. I have been informed by the First Defendant, and verily believe, that shortly after the death of the deceased a local estate agent estimated the value of "Scarr View" at £52,000. From my knowledge of property prices in the area I believe that the estimate may well be correct.

4. By her Will dated 27th July 1981 the deceased appointed the First Defendant, myself and the Third Defendant as her executors and trustees. She gave 5 pieces of jewellery to the Plaintiff, and a pair of silver candlesticks and an oak chest to the Third Defendant. In order to save expense none of these items has been valued, but of course that can be done should the Court so require. She gave pecuniary legacies of £500 each to Caddy Jellyby of 11, Thavies Inn, London EC1 and Lady Honoria Deadlock of Chesney Wold, near Boston, Lincolnshire. All the residue of her property after

payment of her debts and funeral and testamentary expenses and any capital transfer tax or other duties she gave to the First Defendant. By reason of the spouse exemption, there is no capital transfer tax to pay.

5. All the beneficiaries of the deceased's estate are of full age and capacity.

6. The deceased held no general power of appointment over any property, and made no nomination or *donatio mortis causa* of property within section 8 of the Inheritance (Provision for Family and Dependants) Act, 1975. Nor did she hold any property on a joint tenancy, apart from "Scarr View." Nor did she make any disposition, or enter into any contract, within sections 10 or 11 of the said Act.

7. I know of no facts or matters which might affect the exercise of the Court's powers under the Act, apart from the following:

(i) the deceased and the Defendant executed Wills in similar terms on 27th July 1981. I took instructions for these from them together, and they executed them together, so each knew the terms of the other's Will.

(ii) I happened to meet the deceased socially a few weeks before she died. She told me about the financial difficulties which the Plaintiff's husband was experiencing, and expressed an intention of helping the Plaintiff and her family. However, she remarked to me that the help she could give was limited, because the First Defendant had retired.

SWORN etc.

7. Draft Affidavit by Beneficiary

[*Heading as precedent 5, above*]

I, FREDERICK CHARLES JARNDYCE of "Scarr View," Rowbotham Lane, Ghylldale, Yorkshire, retired research chemist, make oath and say as follows:

1. I am the First Defendant herein. I have read the affidavit sworn on ___ by my stepdaughter Anne Mary Skimpole, the Plaintiff herein, and make this affidavit in answer thereto. I can depose to the truth of the facts and matters set forth in this affidavit from my own knowledge, except where the contrary appears, and my means of knowledge sufficiently appear herein.

2. As the Plaintiff deposes in her affidavit, I am one of the executors of the Will of my late wife, the above named Annabel Jarndyce. I have read a draft of the affidavit which is to be sworn by the Second Defendant herein as an independent executor, setting out the matters required to be placed before the Court by virtue of Order 99, rule 5 of the Rules of the Supreme Court, and can confirm that they are accurate.

3. I can and do confirm the truth of the facts set out in paragraphs 1 to 8 inclusive of the Plaintiff's affidavit. I have no reason to doubt the facts in paragraphs 10 and 11 thereof. With regard to paragraph 9 thereof, I was the joint owner of "Scarr View" with the deceased, and am informed by the Second Defendant and verily believe that I am now the sole owner thereof, by virtue of the "right of survivorship."

4. Unfortunately paragraph 12 of the Plaintiff's affidavit shows that she has formed a very misleading view of my financial position. My income consists of the state retirement pension, now £35.80 a week; about £500 a year from my savings; and my pension from International Pharmaceuticals Limited. In the last tax year that pension was £11,565. It is not index linked, but increases automatically by 3 per cent a year to give some protection against inflation. In the past few years International Pharmaceuticals has made very good profits (to a great extent, I believe, because of the efforts in previous years of the research team of which I was a member), and has been able to make gratuitous payments into the pension fund, so that pensions have not fallen very far behind inflation (although they have to some extent). However, there is no guarantee that these payments can or will continue.

5. My only assets are my home, "Scarr View" and about £15,000 in capital.

   (a) Shortly after the deceased died, in December 1984, a local estate agent inspected "Scarr View" for me, and estimated its value as £52,000. I thought this was low, and told him so, but he said that he could not give a higher figure, for two reasons. First, "Scarr View" was pre-eminently a home for a retired couple in easy financial circumstances, and was not very suitable for a young or retired couple with less money, nor very suitable for a family. Secondly, the comparatively large sums which had been spent on its fixtures and fittings did not produce a proportionate increase in its value.

   (b) My capital consist of the following:

4,000 £1 shares in International
Pharmaceuticals Ltd.   £12,015.75

National Savings Certificates,
nominal value £2,000

Bank Current account at the
Capital &Counties Bank,
Ghylldale   £1,000 approximately

My expenditure is as follows:

Rates	£ 50 per calendar month (£600 a year)
Food	£120 per month
Miscellaneous household expenses	£ 10 per month
Clothing	£ 15 per month
Motor expenses	£ 70 a month (excluding depreciation)
Holidays	£160 per month (a little less than £2,000 a year)
Gas	£ 40 per month
Electricity	£ 9 per month
House and contents insurance	£ 10 per month
BUPA subscription	£ 34.17 per month (£410 a year)
Miscellaneous	£135 per month approximately
	653.17 per calendar month

7. I wish to give some information about my financial arrangements with the deceased. During our marriage I paid all our regular expenses. These included food and clothing for the two of us, and for the Plaintiff and the Third Defendant while they were dependant upon us; all the household expenses, including the rates and mortgage instalments; and the cost of buying and running the family car. I also paid all the school fees of the Plaintiff and the First Defendant, and some part of the cost of our family holidays. The deceased paid the remainder of our holiday expenses, and spent money on family luxuries. At the end of each year part of her earnings was still unspent, and she used to save that part. We deliberately adopted this arrangement so that we did not become dependant upon the Deceased's income for any important item of regular expenditure. However, it had the result that her savings became larger than mine; in fact until I retired my savings were limited to a few shares in International Pharmaceuticals Limited which I bought under an employees' share option scheme. I did not worry about the discrepancy between our savings, because like

many if not most couples who are happily married I thought that our property was ours rather than mine or hers. The deceased thought the same. We had made our Wills at the same time, and in similar terms, that is to say with some small legacies, and outright gift, of everything else to each other.

8. When I retired I received a lump sum of £20,000 under my employer's pension scheme. I spent part of that sum on the building of "Scarr View," because we spent more on its building than we received from the sale of our home in Coketown. Most of the rest of the money went on carpets, curtains, and some new pieces of furniture. Only six or seven thousand pounds were left.

9. I have a great deal of sympathy with the Plaintiff, her husband and children, in the financial misfortune that has befallen them. I am concerned about their children's education, and before I had any idea that these proceedings were contemplated I had mentioned the possibility of my paying Sally's fees for her remaining time at Coketown Girls Grammar School—some four years. I still have that possibility in mind, subject to the result of this litigation. So far as John's education is concerned, he is at the local primary school, and I think he could perfectly well go on at 11, with most of his school friends, to Coketown Manor High School, a nearby secondary school maintained by the local authority, where there are of course no fees, and which enjoys a very good reputation. Moreover I do not see why the Plaintiff should not be able to earn more by part time work, even if necessary by taking a full time job. Nor am I as pessimistic as she and her husband appear to be about her husband's prospects of obtaining some kind of employment. I put the Plaintiff to proof of the efforts she and her husband have made to increase their income in these ways.

10. I am advised and verily believe that the Court does not have power under the Inheritance (Provision for Family and Dependants) Act 1975 to make an order in favour of Sally or John. I submit that no order ought to be made in the Plaintiff's favour with a view to helping Sally and John, for two reasons. First, there can be no guarantee that the Plaintiff will in fact apply for Sally or John's benefit any money ordered to be paid to her. Secondly, although I still intend to help Sally, circumstances may change in the next few years. For example, I may become chronically ill, or she may win a scholarship, or decide to leave school before she is 18.

11. More generally, I submit that the Court ought not to make any order in the Plaintiff's favour, especially because of my long and happy marriage to the deceased; the money I spent on the education, upbringing and maintenance of the Plaintiff and the

Third Defendant; and the fact that the Plaintiff and her family have enough money for their necessary expenses.

SWORN, etc.

8. Draft Calderbank Letter

To Messrs Tulkinghorn & Co., solicitors,
   7/10 Industrial Avenue
   Coketown
   Yorkshire   Without Prejudice except as to Costs

Dear Sirs,

Annabel Jarndyce deceased

As you know, we act both in the administration of the estate of the above named deceased, and for the First Defendant in his personal capacity.

We are advised by Counsel that your client's application for financial provision out of the estate of the above named deceased is misconceived, and will almost certainly be dismissed. Moreover your client may well be ordered to pay the costs of the Defendants as personal representatives, and the First Defendant's costs as beneficiary. In her Opinion Counsel refers to *Re Coventry* [1980] Ch.461.

However, the First Defendant, and indeed the Second and Third Defendants, are very unhappy that this family dispute has arisen. Moreover, the First Defendant has always been minded to help your client's daughter Sally complete her education at Coketown Girls Grammar School. Therefore the First Defendant proposes that your client brings these proceedings to an end on the following terms:

1. The First Defendant would execute a deed of covenant to pay to or for the benefit of Sally for 4 years such sum as after the deduction of basic rate income tax thereon would leave the sum of £1,500.

2. Your client would receive £1,000 out of the estate of the deceased for her own use and benefit absolutely.

3. The costs of your client of and incidental to her application (to be taxed if not agreed) would be paid out of the estate on the common fund basis.

We think it is reasonable to ask your client to give us her answer to this proposal within 28 days. Should she accept, the matter will have to remain technically "subject to contract" until the order is actually made, to allow for any points our Counsel or your Counsel may have on the drafting of it.

If your client does not accept these proposals, we reserve the right to refer to this letter when the question of costs is argued at the trial. In this connection we of course refer you to *Calderbank* v. *Calderbank* [1976] Fam.93 and *Cutts* v. *Head* [1984] Ch.290.

We await hearing from you as soon as possible but in any event within 28 days.

                                                        Yours faithfully,

Appendix 5

Part I

Reported cases under the Inheritance (Provision for Family and Dependants) Act 1975

Re Adams, Adams v. Adams, Fam. Div. and C.A. July 22, 1981, C.A. transcripts 81/299 and 81/311.

The applicants were the widow of the deceased and his minor child by her. The Court of Appeal was only concerned with their application to apply out of time. The applications were only 19 days late, the estate had not been distributed, the executors had always known of the intended applications, and the widow at least would be severely prejudiced if she were to be barred from claiming under the Act. However, the delay appeared to be the‑ fault of the applicants' solicitor and therefore the Judge at first instance refused leave, relying on *Re Salmon,* below. The Court of Appeal allowed the widow's appeal, considering that her possible claim in negligence against her solicitor was not decisive in the circumstances of the case.

(The second Court of Appeal transcript was concerned with costs. The Court of Appeal exercised the Court's summary jurisdiction to order the applicants' solicitor to pay the costs thrown away as a result of his conduct.)

Re Besterman [1984] Ch. 458, Ch.D., C.A.

The applicant was the widow of the deceased, who had been married to her for about 17 years. They had no children. He died in 1976. His net estate was worth nearly £1,500,000. By his will he left the applicant his personal chattels, and a life interest in £100,000 nominal War Stock, producing an income of about £3,500. The remainder of his estate was devoted to charitable purposes of an academic nature. In 1980 an interim order was made for a capital sum of £75,000, income of £11,500 a year, and a payment of £3,500 a year for the upkeep of the former matrimonial home, until it was sold. This was to be additional to the entitlement under the will. The applicant had very little money of her own. She used the £75,000 to buy a dwelling-house. The charities accepted that reasonable financial provision had not been made and the trial judge made an order which enlarged the life interest in the War Loan to an absolute interest; gave her a further £110,000 as capital to produce, should an annuity be purchased, a net spendable income of £17,000 a year; a further lump sum of £15,000 as a precautionary reserve; and allowed the retention of the dwelling-house and any surplus from the interim £75,000. The Court of Appeal increased the total capital awarded from £125,000 to £275,000, for three reasons. First, reasonable financial provision for a spouse was not restricted to reasonable financial provision for maintenance, so a straightforward annuity calculation was not necessarily appropriate. Secondly, there ought to be a greater allowance for unforeseeable contingencies. Thirdly, more weight ought to be given to the provision which the applicant might have expected to get if the marriage had ended in divorce.

Re Beaumont [1980] Ch. 444, Ch.D.

The Plaintiff claimed as a person maintained by the deceased under section 1(1)(*e*). The Court struck out his application, on the ground that he had not shown that the deceased had assumed responsibility for his maintenance. In *Jelley* v. *Iliffe*, below, the Court of Appeal overruled the principle of the decision on this crucial point, holding that the fact of maintenance will generally imply an assumption of responsibility for maintenance. However, the Court of Appeal in that later case agreed with the Judge on the other points of the construction of the 1975 Act which he discussed. Those points are set out in the note of *Jelley* v. *Iliffe*, below.

Brill v. *Proud* (1984) 14 Fam. Law 59, C.A., C.A. transcript 83/369

The applicant was the former wife of the deceased. They had married in 1962 and had been divorced in 1978. By a consent order made on the divorce the matrimonial home and its contents, worth £12,750, were transferred to the applicant for £1,000. There were no maintenance payments. In 1980 the deceased died, leaving his estate of £12,000 to a neighbour and mutual friend. The bulk of the estate was made up of money from an insurance policy kept up by the deceased's employers. The applicant alleged that the deceased had deliberately failed to disclose the existence of this policy on the divorce. The trial judge dismissed the application, and the Court of Appeal affirmed the trial judge. The total costs were £7,500. The applicant was legally aided throughout, and the beneficiary from February 3, 1983. The Court of Appeal expressed concern at this amount of costs, and observed that it was the duty of practitioners to inform the Legal Aid authorities of the likely effect of costs on the estate. The beneficiary was awarded her costs from the Legal Aid Fund in respect of her costs of the appeal until the date she herself obtained legal aid. The beneficiary's costs at first instance came out of the estate, but not the applicant's costs.

Re Bunning [1984] Ch. 480, Ch.D

The applicant was the widow of the deceased. They had married in 1963, when he was 56 and she 34. She helped him in his business, giving up her own employment and its pension prospects in order to do so, until he retired in 1971. Between 1968 and 1973 he gave her money and assets totalling £47,814. She left him in 1978, in circumstances which led the Court to refuse to blame her. He died in 1982, leaving a net estate which was worth £237,000 at the time of the hearing. Most of it he gave to charities. The applicant had total assets of about £98,000, and was able to do part-time work at least. She had the state widow's pension, and the income from her investments. The Court considered that the deceased would have been ordered to pay her £36,000, had the marriage been ended at the date it was by divorce rather than death. However, that could not limit the provision she ought to have, and the Court awarded her £60,000, payable out of the gifts to the charities. The Court stated that it was impossible to demonstrate by any deductive process that this was the right figure, but its rightness was confirmed by the fact that it would achieve a rough equality between the assets of the spouses; that it was comparable with the life interest in residue which the deceased had in 1979 thought a reasonable provision to make for the applicant; and that it would enable the applicant to buy the cottage which she hoped to buy, and also provide some more income, and a reserve for contingencies.

Re Cairnes (1982) 12 Fam. Law 177, Fam. Div.

In this case the Court held that the death benefits payable under a private pension scheme did not fall into the residue of the deceased's estate. However, the somewhat brief report suggests that the benefits might have done so under the rules of the scheme in question, had the facts been different.

Re Callaghan [1985] Fam. 1, Fam. Div.

The applicant applied as a person treated by the deceased as a child of the family of the deceased in relation to a marriage of the deceased. His father had been killed on active service in 1943. Shortly thereafter his father's father gave his mother a house, in which he and his mother lived. In 1950, when he was about 13, the deceased came there as a lodger. Some later the deceased and the applicant's mother began to live together as man and wife, and by 1953 they and the applicant were living together as a family, the deceased treating the applicant as his own son. In 1972, when the applicant was 35 and himself married, his mother married the deceased. In 1973 they moved to Basingstoke in order to be near the applicant and his family, and his mother bought a house there. She transferred it into the joint names of herself and the deceased. She died intestate in May 1980, and all her property passed to the deceased. The applicant and his wife looked after the deceased, who was very ill, and he died intestate in August 1980. On one occasion during that time the deceased wanted to go to a solicitor and make a will, but the applicant would not let him, because he was frail and tired. His estate of about £31,000 passed to his three sisters in Ireland, with whom he had a fond but not intimate relationship. Their means were modest. The applicant had an income of about £7,850 a year and his wife one of about £3,900. They had no capital. They had decided to buy their council house, at a cost of £13,250. The Court held that the treatment as a child of the family in relation to a marriage was not restricted to treatment as a minor or dependant child, so the applicant was qualified to apply. The Court awarded him a lump sum of £15,000, being influenced by the source of the deceased's estate, and the close relationship of the applicant with the deceased.

Re Chatterton, Chatterton v. Chatterton's Executors Fam. Div. and C.A. November 1, 1978, C.A. transcript 78/660

The applicants were the widow and minor child of the deceased. The widow and the deceased had married in November 1971, and separated in March 1972. The child was born in May 1972. The deceased made some voluntary payments of £5 a week for the child's maintenance, but never saw her or knew her name. By his will he left a net estate of £17,000. The widow took nothing; he gave the child a one quarter share contingent on attaining 18. The other three quarters went to charities. The trial judge awarded the widow a lump sum of £1,000, and increased the child's share to a half, contingent as before. There was an appeal on behalf of the child, on the ground that her share should be larger, and not contingent. The Court of Appeal dismissed the appeal, but made no order as to the costs of the child in the Court of Appeal.

Re Christie [1979] Ch. 168, Ch.D.

The applicant was the adult son of the deceased. By her will made in 1963 she left all her interest in one dwelling-house to her daughter, all her interest in another dwelling-house to the applicant, and her residue between them equally. In 1971 she gave all her interest in the first house to her daughter. In November 1976 she sold the second house, buying a third house to live in. She died shortly afterwards and the gift of the second house to the applicant was adeemed. The Court considered the terms of the 1975 Act, and the meaning of "maintenance." The Court found that the deceased had the intention at all times right up to her death that her daughter would have her interest in one house and the applicant in the other, and ordered that the third house be transferred to the applicant. (The authority of this decision is very doubtful in view of the remarks made about it in *Re Coventry*, below.)

Re Clark [1981] C.L.Y. 2884

The applicant was the former wife of the deceased, and the defendant was his widow and administratrix. The Court refused to order the defendant to swear an affidavit as to her means (as distinct from the assets of the estate). The case is only noted in Current Law on this point.

Re Coventry [1980] Ch. 461, Ch.D. and C.A.

The applicant was the adult son of the deceased, who died intestate leaving an estate of about £12,000. The whole of it passed to his widow, the mother of the applicant. The deceased and his widow had married in 1927, and separated in 1957. Both she and the applicant were comparatively poor; her income consisted of her old age pension and supplementary benefit, totalling £26.76 a week, and his of about £52 a week net earnings. He sought a lump sum of about £7000 as a deposit on a house or flat. The trial judge dismissed his application, and that decision was affirmed by the Court of Appeal. The judgments contain important general observations about the jurisdiction under the Act.

Re Crawford (1983) 4 F.L.R. 273, Fam. Div.

The applicant was the former wife of the deceased. They had married in 1943, and were divorced in 1968, in which year the deceased married his second wife. A consent order was made in the divorce proceedings whereby the deceased was to pay the applicant one third of his gross salary, less the mortgage interest and insurance payments for the former matrimonial home, in which the applicant remained. In 1975 the former matrimonial home was sold, and a smaller house was bought for the applicant as her unincumbered property. The deceased's income increased but he refused to pay a third of that increased income to the applicant. In September 1979 he retired, receiving a pension, and a lump sum of £69,767. He paid the lump sum into a joint account in the name of himself and his second wife. In November 1979 the applicant started proceedings to obtain a lump sum as a "clean break," but in January 1980 the deceased died. As a result of his death his second wife and his minor children by her received substantial pensions from his employer, and his second wife in addition a lump sum of £72,402. By his will the deceased divided his estate of £30,892 between his son by the applicant, his second wife, and his two children by his second wife. The applicant had £1,500 capital, in addition to her dwelling-house, and was receiving supplementary benefit; she was 59 and could not be expected to work. The court exercised its power under section 9 and awarded her a lump sum of £35,000 out of the deceased's share of the money in the joint account. The Court made a number of observations on the family provision jurisdiction, and in particular it refused to regard *Re Eyre*, below, as establishing a general proposition that reasonable financial provision under the 1975 Act is the same as periodical payments during life if those payments were either agreed or fixed by the Court.

Re Dennis [1981] 2 All E.R. 140, Ch.D.

The applicant was the adult son of the deceased by his first wife. The net estate was worth some £2,500,000. The applicant had received a gift worth £90,000 and other substantial gifts from the deceased during his life, but had dissipated them. By the Will the applicant was given certain small personal chattels, and a legacy of £10,000; the will also gave £30,000 to the trustees of a settlement under which the applicant had a protected life interest. The great bulk of the estate was given to the deceased's second wife and his two children by her. The deceased's first wife had applied for provision, and her application was pending. The applicant was 38 years old, had neither income nor capital and was unemployed. He applied for provision two years and one month after the death of the deceased; part but not all of the delay was unexplained. He sought no more than the sum required to pay the capital transfer tax on the gift worth £90,000. The Court considered *Re Salmon*, below, and *Re Stone*, below, and held that the applicant had to show that he had an arguable case before the Court would extend the six month time limit. The provision of money to pay the capital transfer tax would not be maintenance (although the payment of debts may be maintenance in some circumstances). Therefore permission to apply out of time was refused.

Re Dymott, Spooner v. *Carroll* Fam. Div. and C.A., December 15, 1980; C.A. transcript 80/942

The applicant claimed as a person maintained by the deceased under section 1(1)(*e*). In 1975 she and he had begun a relationship in which they spent a great deal of time together, sharing holidays and other things such as housekeeping. However, they each maintained themselves out of their earnings and, apparently, kept their own dwelling-houses. Between March and August 1978 the applicant did not work and the deceased paid her £10 per week. In August 1978 the deceased had a heart attack, and thereafter he and the applicant lived on their respective state benefits. The deceased died in July 1979. The trial judge held that the applicant was not qualified to apply, because she had not been maintained by the deceased immediately before his death. The Court of Appeal dismissed her appeal; one Lord Justice observed that the "norm of the relationship" was one of no maintenance. However the Court of Appeal observed that claims under the Act ought to be dealt with immediately on the merits, and time and money not spent on applications to strike out.

Escritt, Re, Escritt, v. *Escritt* Fam. Div and C.A., October 15, 1981, C.A. transcript 81/396; (1982) 3 F.L.R. 280

The applicant was the widow of the deceased. They had been married for a long time, but had parted in 1964. In 1973 the deceased made a will stating that he had made no provision for the applicant thereby because he had already done so, by transferring to her a house (in which she also had an interest) and giving her £1,000. As a result of a short unsuccessful reconciliation in 1975 she lost her job and was allegedly unable to get so good a job again. In April 1977, after the death of the deceased, she decided not to make a claim under the Act, largely because of the family disharmony it would cause. Later, when she was some three years out of time, she sought to make a claim, on the ground that circumstances had changed. The estate had not been distributed. The trial judge posed the question: if, after a full understanding of the nature and prospect of success of a claim available for a dependant against the estate of a deceased under the 1974 Act, that dependant decides not to pursue the claim but at some time later on through supervening circumstances reverses that decision and decides to make a claim, ought the Court to permit that claim to be made irrespective of the length of time which had elapsed, save only that no distribution had taken place? He held that the applicant's case was not strong enough to cause the Court to waive the time limit. The Court of Appeal dismissed the applicant's appeal.

Re Freeman [1984] 1 W.L.R. 1419, Ch.D.

This case is only reported on the question of the meaning of the word "representation" in section 4 of the Act. Probate of a will which made provision for the applicant, the deceased's mistress, had been granted in September 1979, but that grant was revoked in May 1983 on the ground that the will had not been properly executed. On August 23, 1983 letters of administration were granted to the Defendant, the deceased's mother, as the person entitled on intestacy. The Court held that "representation" meant effective or valid representation, so that the six month period ran from August 23, 1983.

Re Fricker (1982) 3 F.L.R. 228, Fam. Div.

An order made by consent in 1977 against the estate of a deceased former husband provided that his former wife, the applicant, should have periodical payments of £2,000 a year less tax and a modest lump sum, and should be entitled to live in a dwelling-house purchased by trustees from the estate of the deceased. The applicant alleged that her income had become insufficient by reason of inflation. She sought a variation of the order, whereby the dwelling-house would be vested in her, so that she could convey it to an insurance company subject to a life tenancy, and buy an annuity with the monies realised. The Court held that it had no power to vary the 1977 order in the manner sought. Under section 6(6) of the 1975 Act an order for variation could only affect property which was applicable for the making of periodical payments. The dwelling-house was not such property.

Re Fullard [1982] Fam. 42, Fam Div. and C.A.

The applicant was the former wife of the deceased. They had married in 1938, and were divorced in 1976. Both had worked during the marriage. On the divorce the applicant paid the deceased £4,500 cash from her life savings, and he conveyed his interest in the former matrimonial home to her. By his Will the deceased left all his estate, consisting mainly of the cash from the Plaintiff, to another lady, with whom he had lived (as a lodger and friend only) since the divorce. The financial circumstances of the applicant and the beneficiary were both modest. The Court of first instance dismissed the application, and the Court of Appeal affirmed that decision. The judgments in the Court of Appeal contain important observations about the jurisdiction under the Act. In particular, the view of the Court was that, with wide powers of financial provision and property adjustment now available on divorce, the number of cases in which a former spouse can claim on death is reduced.

Ormrod L.J. said that they would be comparatively few. This is especially relevant where the estate is small. By way of exception, a claim might be justified when there had been periodical payments for a long time, or when a substantial capital sum was unlocked by the death of the deceased.

Re Haig, Powers v. Haig (1979) 129 N.L.J. 420, Ch.D.

The applicant, 73 years old, claimed as a person maintained by the deceased under section 1(1)(*e*). She and the deceased had lived together as man and wife for the three years before his death. By his will he left the whole of his net estate of £57,000 to his son. The Court stated that applicant's assets were fully sufficient to enable her to live, provided she lived rent free. Therefore the Court ordered the sale of the deceased's house, and the purchase of another house (apparently for the occupation of the applicant during her life).

Re Harmsworth [1982] C.L.Y. 3388, Ch.D.

This case is only reported on a preliminary point of the deceased's domicile. He was held to have retained his domicile of origin.

Harrington v. Gill (1983) 4 F.L.R. 265, Fam. Div and C.A.

The applicant claimed as a person maintained by the deceased under section 1(1)(*e*). In November 1971, when she was about 64, she left her council flat to live with the deceased in the house which he owned. He was then about 69. She kept on the tenancy of her flat, only giving it up after the death of the deceased. The deceased paid all the household bills, without any contribution from the applicant. He died intestate in July 1979, leaving a net estate of £65,000, of which £22,000 represented the value of the house. The sole beneficiary was the deceased's daughter, a married lady in her 40s, of a reasonably comfortable financial position. The applicant had capital of about £1,400, and her state pension. The trial judge found that the applicant was qualified to apply under section 1(1)(*e*). He awarded her a lump sum of £5,000, and the income of another £5,000 for her life. The Court of Appeal did not disturb that award, but in addition settled the house on the applicant upon trust for sale for her life, with remainder to the daughter.

Re Homer, Rann v. Jackson Fam. Div and C.A. November 16, 1978, C.A. transcript 78/723

The applicant was the adult daughter of the deceased, 54 years old, married and in no especial need. The deceased's net estate was valued at £23,000. By his will he gave £2,000 to the applicant, one or two other small legacies, and the residue to his unmarried daughter. The applicant had capital of £17,000, and earned about £3,000 a year. The trial judge dismissed the claim, and the Court of Appeal dismissed the appeal.

Jelley v. *Iliffe* [1981] Fam. 128, Fam. Div and C.A.

The applicant claimed as a person maintained by the deceased in the period immediately before her death, under section 1(1)(*e*). The Defendants were her three children, the beneficiaries under her Will, one of whom was her executor. Relying on *Re Beaumont*, above, they sought to strike out the application on the ground that no assumption of responsibility for maintenance was shown. They succeeded before the District Registrar and the trial judge, but the Court of Appeal allowed the applicant's appeal, leaving the application to go to trial. The Court of Appeal, disagreeing with part of the judgment in *Re Beaumont*, held that the bare fact of maintenance would generally raise a presumption that responsibility for maintenance had been assumed. Therefore the application could not be struck out without a hearing. However, the Court of Appeal agreed with *Re Beaumont* in that

(1) the deeming provision in section 1(3) exhaustively or exclusively defines what section 1(1)(*e*) means by "being maintained," and does not extend it.

(2) In considering whether a person is being maintained "immediately before the death of the deceased" it is the settled basis or general arrangement between the parties which has to be looked at.

(3) The words "otherwise than for full valuable consideration" do not apply only to full valuable consideration under a contract, but apply whenever full valuable consideration is given, whether under contract or otherwise.

The judgment contains other general observations of importance, including one that provision to an applicant of rent-free accommodation is a substantial contribution to reasonable needs.

Re Kennedy [1980] C.L.Y. 2820, Shoreditch County Court

This case is only noted in Current Law on an anti-avoidance point under section 10 of the Act. The applicant was the widow of the deceased, whom she had married in 1941. In 1940 he had deserted her to live with a mistress, and in March 1977 he had transferred his house to himself and the mistress jointly. In April 1977 the applicant petitioned for divorce. Before a decree was granted the deceased died, leaving all his estate to his mistress, who herself died intestate a few months later. The County Court Judge held that it was not essential for the applicant to show that the deceased had the Act in his mind when he made the impugned transaction, but there had to be evidence that he intended to defeat a claim made after his death against his estate. There being no such evidence, the application under section 10 was dismissed.

Re Kirby (1981) Fam. Law 210, Fam. Div.

This case is only reported on an application to strike out. The applicant claimed as a person maintained by the deceased under section 1(1)(*e*). He had lived with the deceased for some 35 years. She died intestate, leaving a net estate of £6,942.49 which passed to her children. The administrator, one of the children, sought to strike out the claim. Both the deceased and the applicant had worked during their cohabitation, and thereafter enjoyed pensions. The Court considered that there had been mutual dependency with varying degrees of contributions throughout their joint lives. The administrator had shown neither that the contributions were equally balanced, nor that the balance of dependency would tip in favour of the dependence of the deceased upon the applicant. Therefore the claim would not be struck out.

Kourkey v. *Lusher* (1982) 12 Fam. Law 86, Fam. Div.

The applicant had been the deceased's mistress intermittently over a period of 10 years, and claimed as a person maintained by him under section 1(1)(*e*). Throughout his relationship with the applicant the deceased had maintained contact with his wife. The relationship began in 1969, but was deteriorating from 1972. In July 1979 the deceased went on holiday with his wife, and told her he would be returning to her for good. At the end of the holiday he did not resume cohabitation with the applicant. He died shortly afterwards. The Court held that the applicant was not qualified to apply, apparently because of the deceased's failure to resume cohabitation with her, and the indications he had given that he had abandoned all responsibility for her. Even had she been qualified to apply for provision, the Court would apparently have refused an order on the facts. The Court would not have made an order under section 9 in respect of the matrimonial home, and apart from his share in that the estate was only worth £1,931. (The reports of the case are somewhat unclear on this latter aspect of the matter.)

Re Kozdrach, Sobesto v. *Farren* Interlocutory hearing in C.A. November 9, 1979, C.A. transcript 77/755; general note at [1981] Conv. 224, Fam. Div.

The applicant, who had been living with the deceased as his wife, applied as a person maintained by him under section 1(1)(*e*). The gross estate was worth about £55,000 and passed under the intestacy rules to the deceased's sister in Poland. Because the Court might at the substantive hearing order the deceased's dwelling-house to be transferred to the applicant, the Court of Appeal restrained its sale until then. At the substantive hearing in the Family Division, the Court awarded the applicant a lump sum of £18,000 and ordered that she could within six months apply for a transfer of the dwelling-house provided she paid £9,000. The value of the dwelling-house was £22,500 at death, but £28,000 at the time of the hearing.

Re Leach [1985] 3 W.L.R. 413, Ch.D.

The applicant applied under section 1(1)(*d*) of the Act as a person treated as a child of the family in relation to a marriage to which the deceased was a party. The deceased was the applicant's stepmother, having married the applicant's father in 1960, when the applicant was 32, and self supporting. The evidence suggested that the applicant's father had provided part of the purchase price of the matrimonial home of himself and the deceased, although it was conveyed into the deceased's sole name. The applicant's father died in 1974, leaving his estate of £3,000 to the deceased. The applicant had enjoyed a close relationship with her father and the deceased during the marriage, and after her father's death her relationship with the deceased became even closer. The deceased died intestate in 1981, and her estate of £35,000 passed to her two sisters and brother. The applicant was 55, unmarried, and earned £6,250 a year. Her only capital assets were a half interest in her home, jointly owned with a close woman friend, and some small savings. She had substantial liabilities. Taking into account the source of finance for the matrimonial home, the close relationship between the applicant and the deceased, the absence of evidence that the deceased intended to die intestate, and the applicant's financial position, the court of first instance considered that reasonable financial provision had not been made. It awarded a lump sum of £19,000, which would enable the applicant to pay off a large part of her indebtedness, and thus release additional income for maintenance before and during her retirement. The Court of Appeal upheld this order on appeal. It considered that treatment after the end of the marriage could be relevant in applications under section 1(1)(*d*), as could treatment when the child was an adult.

Re Lewis, Lewis v. *Lynch* Ch.D and C.A., March 13, 1980, C.A. transcript 80/158

The applicant was the widow of the deceased. They had married in 1968. He had three children by a previous marriage, and she had one. They had one further child. In 1971 he made a will giving her two cars and his personal effects, an annuity of £2,000, and £10,000 to provide a house for her widowhood. He died in 1974. His trustees, in breach of trust, spent £18,000 rather than £10,000 on a house for her. She had a net annual income of £3,400. The available liquid assets in the estate amount to £50,000. The trial judge confirmed her in the occupation of the house during her widowhood, and made her a tenant for life thereof. The Court of Appeal did not disturb this, but in addition allowed her appeal by giving her a further lump sum of £10,000, supplied by taking £2,500 out of the gifts to each child of the deceased in the will. The Court of Appeal allowed the appeal to this extent because it considered that the trial Judge had compensated for inflation insofar as it had rendered the provision for living accommodation inadequate, but not in so far as it had rendered inadequate the provision for income.

Re Longley [1981] C.L.Y. 2885, Ch.D.

This case is only noted in Current Law on the question of extension of time. The Court refused to extend time for an application because, *inter alia*, there was a claim against the applicant's solicitors for negligence. (This must now be read in the light of *Re Adams*, above.)

Malone v. *Harrison* [1979] 1 W.L.R. 1353, Fam. Div.

The Plaintiff, aged 38 in 1979, applied as a person maintained by the deceased under section 1(1)(*e*) of the Act. She had been his mistress from 1965 until his death in 1977, and he had supported her during that time, although they had never lived together as man and wife. He already had a "de facto spouse." He left a net estate, after capital transfer tax and administration expenses, of about £480,000. The Court estimated that the applicant had received at least £4,000 a year from the deceased during their relationship, and sought to enable her to have, through income and capital, the same sum. She had obtained employment at £2,000 a year, and had free capital of £23,000, derived from the deceased. The Court used these figures to arrive at the award to her in a way similar to that used in calculating damages for personal injuries. Assuming an earning capacity until 60, a multiplier of 11 was applied to £2,000, giving £22,000. The applicant's actuarial expectation of life was about 76, so a further period of 16 years had to be covered, and a multiplier of 5 was applied to the multiplicand of £4,000, giving £20,000. The total of the two sums was £42,000. The applicant already had capital resources of £23,000, so the Court awarded the difference, £19,000, although without interest. The Court further directed that the sum should be paid out of the entitlement of the deceased's brother under the Will, and not out of the entitlement of his "de facto spouse."

Re McC (otherwise *C.A.* v. *C.C.*) *The Times*, November 17, 1978; (1979) 9 Fam. Law 26; (1979) 123 S.J. 35, Fam. Div.

The applicants were a woman who had lived with the deceased as his "de facto wife" and her child by him. In 1972 she had begun living with him and his minor child at his home. Their child was born in 1974. He died in 1976, leaving a net estate of between £20,000 and £35,000. Under his will it all went to his minor son. The Court observed that everything pointed to a family unit, and awarded the woman a lump sum of £5,000. The Court further ordered that the balance of the estate should be shared equally between the two children (none of the three reports of this case are especially full or clear).

Nobbs, Re, Midland Bank Trust Co. Ltd. v. *Nobbs* (1981) 131 N.L.J. 342; C.A. June 9, 1980, C.A. transcript 80/372

The applicant was the widow of the deceased. Her application was dismissed at the trial, when she failed to attend it. She appealed. The Court of Appeal ordered her to give security for costs in the sum of £2,000, even though she was legally aided.

Re Pitkin, Barnsley v. *Ward* Ch.D and C.A., January 18, 1980, C.A. transcript 80/19

This case only reached the Court of Appeal on the issue of interim orders under section 5. The applicant appears to have been claiming as a person maintained by the deceased under section 1(1)(e). She had an income of £20 a week and outgoings of £77 a week, and on an interlocutory application the Court of first instance had awarded her £50 a week until a specified time. The Defendant executor appealed from this, but the Court of Appeal dismissed that appeal with costs, and ordered that the interim provision of £50 a week should continue until judgment or further order. The Court of Appeal deprecated appeals from decisions on interim provision under section 5.

Re Portt, Allcorn v. *Harvey* Oxford County Court and C.A. March 25, 1980, C.A. transcript 80/289

The applicant, aged 70, was the daughter of the deceased, who left an estate of £12,000, most of it to her granddaughter. The applicant owned and lived in a cottage worth £11,000, had capital of £10,698, and an income of £2,200 a year. The granddaughter earned £3,000 a year, was married to a husband earning £9,300 a year, and lived with him in their jointly owned house worth £11,000. The deceased left nothing to the applicant for fear she would waste it on litigation. The County Court Judge dismissed her application, and the Court of Appeal dismissed her appeal.

Re Rowlands [1984] F.L.R. 813, C.A.

The applicant was the widow of the deceased. They had married in 1919 and separated in 1938. The estate consisted of farming assets worth over £100,000, which the deceased left to his two sons. The applicant was living with her daughter and son-in-law in their cottage. The trial judge awarded her a lump sum of £3,000. The Court of Appeal dismissed her appeal, holding that the trial judge had properly taken into account her inability to formulate what she required money for, and the intention of the deceased to try to keep the farms together for the benefit of his family in the future.

Re Salmon [1981] Ch. 167, Ch.D.

This case is only reported on the applicant's request for an extension of the six months period for applying. She was the widow of the deceased. Her application was issued some five and a half months after the time limit had expired, largely because of her solicitor's inaction. The Court identified a number of guidelines, although they were plainly not exhaustive. First, the discretion is unfettered. Secondly, the onus lies on the applicant to establish sufficient grounds for taking the case out of the general rule, and depriving those who are protected by it of its benefit. Thirdly, it must be material to consider how promptly and in what circumstances the applicant has sought the permission of the Court after the time limit has expired. Fourthly, it is material whether or not negotiations have been commenced within the time limit, or indeed to some extent after it. Fifthly, it is relevant to consider whether or not the estate has been distributed before the claim has been made or notified. Sixthly, it is relevant to consider whether a refusal to extend the time would leave the claimant without redress against anybody. In the instant case the applicant appeared to have a strong claim against her solicitors, so the sixth guideline was highly relevant and the Court refused the request for an extension of time. (This must now be read in the light of *Re Adams*, above.)

Re Sehota [1978] 3 All E.R. 385, Ch.D.

In this case the Court held that a spouse whose marriage to the deceased was potentially or actually polygamous was qualified to claim as a spouse of the deceased under the Act. The case is only reported on this preliminary point.

Re Snoek (1983) 13 Fam. Law 19, Fam. Div.

The applicant was the widow of the deceased. They married in 1959, and had four children. The deceased had three children by a former wife. Until about 1969 the marriage was happy, but from then onwards it started to fall apart because of the applicant's uncontrollable temper and frequent outbursts of violence. In October 1976 the deceased filed a petition for divorce. He died in October 1980 after a long terminal illness. He left an estate of £40,000. By his Will he gave £7,180 in specific bequests to the three youngest children, and divided the net residue of £30,000 equally between his seven children. The youngest child was under age, and not self supporting. The Court held, although hesitantly in view of the applicant's conduct, that the Will did not make reasonable financial provision for her, and awarded her a lump sum of £5,000. The Court further directed that the gift to the deceased's children by his first marriage, and that to the youngest child, should be held upon trust until the youngest child attained 21, and the income used for his benefit in the meantime.

Stead v. *Stead* [1985] F.L.R. 16, Fam. Div. and C.A.

The applicant was the widow of the deceased. They married in 1957, when she was 55 and he was 63. Both had been married before. During the marriage she made a substantial contribution to the family's finances and welfare. The deceased's estate consisted of the matrimonial home, valued at about £30,000, and liquid assets of about £34,000. His will gave the applicant a life interest in the matrimonial home, she to pay all the outgoings, and a life interest in the sum of £6,000. She had £1,000 capital of her own. The residue was given to his adult children. The trial judge made an order, *inter alia* that:

(1) The applicant be paid a lump sum of £2,500.
(2) The applicant be paid £1,500 a year gross periodical payments.
(3) The trustees should have leave to distribute the sum of £8,000 forthwith.

(4) The applicant be allowed to live in the former matrimonial home under the terms of the will, provided that with her consent the house might be sold and another purchased out of the proceeds of sale for her occupation on the same terms and conditions.
(5) When the applicant no longer wished to reside in any house held under those terms, the trustees should have a discretion to increase the income provision for her out of the retained fund representing the proceeds of sale of any such house.
(6) The applicant should pay the general and water rates in respect of any such house, and be responsible for all internal repairs and decorations, but the trustees should pay the insurance premium and be responsible for all external repairs and decorations on a normal landlord and tenant basis.

The Court of Appeal dismissed the applicant's appeal. She was legally aided, and the Court of Appeal ordered the Legal Aid Fund to pay the respondent defendants' costs of the appeal.

Re Viner [1978] C.L.Y. 3091, Chancery Master

The applicant, who was a widowed sister of the deceased, applied as a person maintained by the deceased under section 1(1)(e). He left a net of estate of £44,210.02 before payment of capital transfer tax. The residuary legatee had been an employee and director of the deceased's private company, and was in comfortable financial circumstances. The applicant had been left in hard financial circumstances by the death of her husband a year before the death of the deceased, and he had reluctantly paid her £5 a week in the six months before his death. Master Chamberlain held that she was qualified to apply, but the fact that the £5 a week had been paid grudgingly ought to be taken into account, and accordingly reasonable financial provision would be restricted to that made by the testator. Because a weekly sum of £5 would adversely affect the applicant's rent and rates rebate, a lump sum of £5,000 was awarded.

Re Wilkinson [1978] Fam 22, Fam. Div.

The applicant was a sister of the deceased. A preliminary point arose as to whether she was qualified to claim, as a person maintained by the deceased under section 1(1)(e). In September 1969 the deceased had persuaded her to give up her employment and live with the deceased, in the deceased's home. The deceased discharged the whole of the household expenses. The applicant did a share, apparently an equal share, of the light housework and cooking. She helped the deceased to dress and was available as a companion. The Court held, with some uncertainty, that she had not given full valuable consideration, and allowed the application to go forward. The case is only reported on this preliminary point.

Williams v. *Roberts* [1984] Fam. Law 210, Fam. Div.

The applicant applied as a person maintained by the deceased under section 1(1)(*e*). They had begun to live together as man and wife in 1969, in a guest house run by the applicant. Over a period of about ten years the deceased helped the applicant to run the guest house, made several lump sum payments to her, and weekly payments towards his board and lodging. In 1977 they became engaged to be married, and planned to buy a retirement home, which would have been in the applicant's name. The deceased died in 1981, leaving his estate of about £100,000 to his two sisters (by a will made in 1962, apparently before he had met the applicant). The Court held that on the facts the applicant was qualified to apply. The Court took into account the retirement planning, the loss of the lump sums and weekly payments, and the nursing of the deceased by the applicant. A lump sum of £20,000 was awarded.

Re Wood (1982) 79 L.S.Gaz 774, Ch.D.

The applicant was the 30-year-old daughter of the deceased. She was severely mentally subnormal, but could appreciate extra comforts and clothing. The deceased died intestate leaving an estate of £26,737.25. £25,000 of that passed to the deceased's husband, the applicant's stepfather. He died within a year, and his estate passed to his son by an earlier marriage. The applicant therefore received only £1,737.25 from the deceased's estate. She had other capital of about £3,519, and an income from state benefits of £1,037 a year. Her father, who was apparently still alive, was without resources. The Court awarded her a lump sum of £15,000.

Part II

Cases under the former legislation

Re Andrews [1955] 1 W.L.R. 1105

This was an application by an unmarried daughter of the testator, who had left her nothing in his will. She was aged 69 at the date of the hearing, and dependent on national assistance. She had left the parental home at the age of 25 or so, to live with a married man. The Court held that she had left in order to set up a permanent home with that man, no doubt relying on him to provide her with the companionship and the protection, financial and otherwise, which she would have had a right to expect from him had they married. It necessarily followed that her father ceased to have any moral obligation to maintain her from the time when it could be postulated that she had set up this permanent relationship. Therefore the application was dismissed. The report does not give the costs order, nor the value of the estate.

Askew v. *Askew* [1961] 1 W.L.R. 725

This was an application by a former wife. Her former husband had been paying her £377 a year less tax at the date of his death. He left his estate (£28,000, less about £5,000 estate duty) to his widow for life, and thereafter to a nephew and three nieces. He made no provision for continuing the periodical payments to the applicant. The parties agreed that she should receive £5.10s.0d a week, and that the costs of the application should come out of the estate, but were unable to agree as to the date from which the payments should be made. The Court held that they should run from the date of the testator's death, even though the former wife might therefore have to repay some of the national assistance she had received in the meantime.

Re Bateman (1941) 85 S.J. 454

The applicant was the widow of the testator, who had left his whole estate of about £500 upon trusts for his minor daughter. The applicant was earning £2 a week but had no property of her own. The Court held that in the circumstances the child had the first claim on the estate, but those circumstances might change, so the application would stand over with liberty to the applicant to restore it not later than six months after the daughter had attained 21, or upon any change of circumstances.

Re Bates [1953] 1 W.L.R. 276

This case was primarily concerned with the statutory limits on the amount of provision awardable, which were contained in the Inheritance (Family Provision) Act 1938 as originally enacted.

Bayliss v. *Lloyds Bank* County Court and C.A., December 9, 1977, C.A. transcript 77/478A

The applicants were the widow and minor daughter of the deceased. She had married him as his second wife in about 1948. He had three young children whom she helped to bring up, and she herself had four children by him. He died in 1970, leaving the three children by his first marriage grown up and well established, and three of his four children by the applicant of full age. By his will he gave specific legacies to all his children, except the youngest, who had not been born at the time of the will. He gave his residue, which included the matrimonial home, to the applicant during widowhood. The net residue was smaller than the deceased must have anticipated, so that on the will as it stood the matrimonial home would have to be sold. The widow's income was modest. The Deputy County Court Judge dismissed her application, but awarded the minor daughter a lump sum. The Court of Appeal allowed the widow's appeal, and ordered that she should have the matrimonial home outright. It was conceded in the light of this that the minor daughter should have no lump sum; the widow would look after her.

Re Beale The Times, June 4, 1964

The applicant was the widower of the testatrix. They had married in 1971, when he was 69 and she was 48. She left her whole estate of about £3,500 to her son by a previous marriage. Its major asset was the former matrimonial home. The Court awarded the applicant £2 a week for life or until remarriage.

Re Bellman [1963] P. 239

The applicant was a former wife of the deceased. She had married him in 1935 and divorced him in 1941. He remarried, and had two children by his second wife, but was divorced by her in 1949. After that he saw a good deal of the applicant, and although she refused to remarry him she gave him much moral support; she gave up a pensionable job in order to accompany him to South Africa on a business trip. At the date of his death she was receiving £350 a year joint lives maintenance from him, and a payment of £350 a year from his company; she had other income totalling about £350 a year, of which £280 came from a part time job as a secretary to a doctor. She had capital of about £3,000. She was 60 years of age and in indifferent health. Her prospects of increasing her earnings were limited, although she was able to increase them to £520 after the death of the deceased. He left his net estate of about £35,000 for the benefit of his two children by his second wife; they were still being educated. The court awarded the applicant £300 a year, less tax, out of the estate.

Re Bidie [1949] Ch. 121

Letters of administration to the estate of the deceased were granted on April 13, 1945. Subsequently a will was found, the grant of letters of administration was revoked, and probate of the will was granted on September 7, 1946. On a preliminary point, the Court of Appeal held that the six-month period for applying under the Inheritance (Family Provision) Act 1938 ran from the probate of the will, and not from the grant of letters of administration. Two members of the Court of Appeal expressed the view that the position would be the same where there were two wills so that, if one was proved and a later one then found, the six month period would run from the proving of the later one.

Re Black The Times, March 25, 1953

The applicant was the daughter and only child of the testator. She was about 64 years old. He left a net estate of about £123,000. Under his will she took his household chattels, and he directed his trustees to make up her income to £1,000 a year gross should the income from the investments he had given her during his lifetime ever fall below that sum. He gave the residue of his estate to charity. The applicant could not earn her own living. The Court said that the case was an unusual one, and was unlikely to be a guide in other cases. It made an award of £1,500 a year from the estate until death or marriage.

Re Blanch [1967] 1 W.L.R. 987

The applicant was the widow of the testator. They had married in 1957, when she was 71 and he 68. The marriage was happy apart from the testator's irrational jealousy. He died in 1965, having left everything to the defendant, his daughter by an earlier marriage. The net estate was worth about £58,000. The applicant's personal income was £315 a year. The Defendant had two minor sons, and her husband earned £2,500 a year. The Court held that a deceased's state of mind might be relevant and material in Inheritance Act cases, and ought to be considered by the Court, although testamentary capacity ought not to be investigated. The order was that the applicant should have £350 a year for two years or until she vacated the former matrimonial home, she not paying an occupation rent in the meantime; and that thereafter she should have £600 a year, less a full occupation rent if she was still in the former matrimonial home.

Re Blight (1946) 96 L.J. 233

This case is only reported on a procedural point. The Court ordered that a beneficiary who was a mental defective ought to be joined as a defendant, and evidence obtained as to what extra comforts could be provided for him in his publicly funded hospital.

Re Bluston [1967] Ch. 615

In this case the Court of Appeal was concerned with the restrictions on the Court's discretion to extend the six-month period for applying under the legislation, which has now been relaxed.

Re Bone [1955] 1 W.L.R. 703

This case was concerned with the restrictions on the Court's discretion to extend the six-month period for applying, which have now been relaxed. The Court refused to extend the time, and the applicant was ordered to pay the costs of all the defendants as between party and party. The first and second defendants received their costs as trustees out of the estate, and any difference between the party and party and the solicitor and own client costs in the case of the third defendant (the beneficiary) was made payable out of the estate.

Re Bonham (1962) 112 L.J. 634

The applicant was the widower of the testatrix, who left a net estate of about £4,800. Under her will the applicant took her personal chattels and £100. The residuary estate, after payment of a legacy of £50, went to her brothers in equal shares. The widower was chiefly dependent upon state benefits. The brothers were in work and had some small capital, but were in precarious health and of advancing age. The Court awarded the applicant an additional £2 a week during widowerhood.

Re Borthwick [1949] Ch. 395

This was an application by a wife and unmarried daughter. The testator had married the wife in 1909, when he had a small income. He went bankrupt in 1925, and left her the same year. Between 1926 and 1939 he acquired considerable wealth, and when he died in 1946 his net residuary estate was about £130,000. At the date of his death he was making his wife a weekly allowance of £3; she knew his circumstances had to some extent improved, but not the extent of the improvement. By his will he gave her an annuity of £250, and settled a legacy of £1,000 on the applicant daughter. The Court held that the wife's receipt of a comparatively small sum by way of maintenance during his life did not prevent her seeking more after his death; that maintenance did not mean mere subsistence; but that the modest circumstances in which she had been living was a matter to be taken into account. On these principles she was awarded £1,000 a year, subject to tax, and the applicant daughter was awarded £100. Although the judgment was given more than 35 years ago, it is still valuable for its comments on the meaning of maintenance, and other aspects of the jurisdiction.

Re Brindle (1941) 192 L.T.J.75

The applicant was the widow of the testator. He left a residuary estate of £2,750, but made no provision for her by his will. She was entitled to a pension, and had a house and some capital, in the form of a claim to a sum of money from the testator's estate. She filed an affidavit in which she stated that, shortly before the testator's death, he had told her that he had done her a wrong, and had expressed a wish to go to a solicitor to alter his will, but she would not let him go, because he was so ill. The Court dismissed her application, because she had a pension, and because the estate was small.

Re Brown (1955) 105 L.J. 169

The applicant was the widow of the testator, who left a net estate of £11,320. By his will he gave a legacy of £2,000 to the plaintiff, and the residue to the children of his first marriage, in fulfilment of a promise to them when they released to him absolutely the residuary estate they took under their mother's will. The Court held that reasonable financial provision had not been made, because the testator's obligation to fulfil his promise to his children did not oust the jurisdiction of the Court, nor was it a decisive circumstance in considering the question of reasonable provision. The Court awarded the applicant some further provision, but the report does not say how much.

Re Brownbridge (1942) 193 L.J.185

The Plaintiff was the widow of the testator. He left his whole net estate, worth some £1,194, to his son. The Court held that the Act did not throw upon a testator the duty to make provision for his dependants, but only gave the Court the right to interfere if it came to the conclusion that the dispositions made were unwarranted. In the instant case the Court dismissed the application, bearing in mind all the circumstances before it, which included a long separation without any attempt by the applicant to claim maintenance: her private means; and the fact that the sole beneficiary was one of the testator's children, who had assisted him in his business.

Re Browne The Times December 14, 1957

The applicant was the widow of the testator, having married him in 1900. She was 73 years old and almost blind. He left his net estate of £2,230 to the woman with whom he had been living since 1937. The

Court awarded the applicant the income which would be earned by the investment of £500, apparently by the purchase of an annuity, which sum appeared to be about £2 a month.

Re Canderton (1970) 114 S.J. 208

The applicant was the widow of the testator. They had married in 1913, and separated in 1919. He went to live with another woman, who died before him, and left him her estate of about £2,850. He left his net estate of about £5,300 to relatives of the other woman. The maintenance of £1 a week which he had been paying the applicant ceased on her death. She was 78 years old, had about £40 capital, a state pension of £4.10s.0d a week and supplementary benefit of £2.6s.0d a week. The Court took into account the claims of both the relatives of the other woman, who were poor, and the Plaintiff's social security position. It made an award of £1 a week and a lump sum of £700.

Re Carter (1968) 112 S.J. 136

The applicant was the widow of the testator. They had separated in 1942, and from then until his death he had paid her £3.10s.0d a week. He left all his net estate of £4,700 to two friends; in December 1965 he had given building society shares worth £3,000 to one of these friends. The evidence showed that he had been largely to blame for the separation. The Court held that although after a matrimonial history of this kind he was not bound to give the whole of his estate to the applicant, he ought to have made specific provision for her; that since he had made a large *inter vivos* gift shortly before his death to the first Defendant it would be right to treat his estate as consisting of both the gifted property and the property left at his death; that the *inter vivos* gift amply fulfilled his desire to benefit his friends; and that accordingly reasonable provision for the applicant was the whole of the net estate.

Re Catmull [1943] Ch. 262

The applicant was the widow of the testator, who left a net estate of less than £2,000. By his will he gave the applicant a life interest in his household goods and personal belongings, and divided all the residue between his six children. The applicant had the widow's pension of 10s. a week, and on attaining 60 would become entitled, in case of need, to a supplementary grant not exceding £1.2s.6d a week. The Court dismissed the application, but in effect ordered all the costs to be paid out of the estate. The Court appears to have been influenced to dismiss the application by the fact that the widow was able to work, and had as a pension "that amount which the state has thought proper to provide for the widows of working men."

Re Charman [1951] 2 T.L.R. 1095

The applicant was the widow of the testator, who left an estate of about £600 or £700. They had married in 1924, and he had left her in 1933. There was one child of the marriage, born in 1925. The testator had paid her £120 a year under a separation agreement until the time of his death. By his will he gave a house to his sister, who was a creditor of his estate, and the residue to the woman with whom he had lived as man and wife since 1946. He left nothing to the applicant, but his former employers granted her a voluntary pension of £2.5s.0d a week. The Court held that the will had not made reasonable financial provision for her, but that, because of the pension, no order ought to be made on the application.

Re Chittenden [1970] 1 W.L.R. 1618

The Court held that an application under the Inheritance (Family Provision) Act 1938 was made when the Summons was issued, rather than when it was served.

Re Clarke [1968] 1 W.L.R. 415

The applicant married the testator in 1961, when she was 36, and he 49. He had previously lived with his mother, and he and the applicant agreed that they should continue to live with her, as a temporary measure. This proved unsatisfactory, and the strain on the applicant was such that after seven months she felt forced to leave. The testator would not come with her. He died in 1964, leaving £1,000 to the Plaintiff and the residue of his estate to his mother. She died intestate in 1965, and her estate, including her rights in the testator's estate, passed to distant relatives. His net estate was worth some £23,000, and his mother's £8,000. The applicant worked as a schoolteacher before, during and after her married life with the testator; at the date of the marriage she was earning about £1,000 a year, and at the date of the proceedings £1,950. At the latter date she was living in her own bungalow. The Court awarded her half the income of the net estate, which half was between £500 and £575 a year, for the rest of her life until her remarriage. This took into account the moral claims upon the testator of both the applicant and his mother; the applicant's failure to claim support from him after their separation; the true reasons for the separation; and the shortness of their married life together.

Re Clayton [1966] 1 W.L.R. 969

The applicant was the widower of the testatrix. They had married in 1950, when he was 41 and she was 51. She died in 1963, leaving a net estate of £1,271 between her sister and her sister's son (subject to a legacy of £10). The Court held that the small size of the estate excluded neither jurisdiction nor full consideration of the application, but was significant in relation to the availability of state aid for the applicant, the extent to which the estate could effectively contribute to his maintenance, and the costs necessarily involved in the application. There was no greater onus of proof on a surviving husband than on a surviving wife. Material facts in the instant case were that the estate was not substantially derived from the applicant; that he was a cripple (although earning); and that the beneficiaries appeared to be well provided for apart from the estate. In the light of this, the applicant was awarded a lump sum of £400.

Re Cole The Times, May 28, 1964

The applicant was the widow of the testator. They had married in 1949, and in 1957 she had left him without any reasonable justification. By his will he gave the residue of his estate to the children of his first marriage. The Court remarked that in the circumstances the applicant would not have been entitled to maintenance before the testator's death, and dismissed her application.

Re Cook mentioned at (1956) 106 L.J. 466

The applicant, aged 70 was the spinster daughter of the deceased, who died intestate, leaving an estate of about £2,500. The persons entitled on intestacy were the applicant and the four other children of the deceased. The Court awarded her a lump sum of £1,000 (to include her share under the intestacy rules).

Re Dorgan [1948] Ch. 366

This case was concerned with the construction of sections 2(1) and 4(1) of the Inheritance (Family Provision) Act 1938. The Court held that section 4(1)(b) merely enabled the Court to make, after the period of six months from the grant, orders in favour of a further dependant when there was already a dependant in receipt of provision under the Act.

Re Doring [1955] 1 W.L.R. 1217

The applicant was the widow of the testator, who had left a net estate of between £28,000 and £30,000. By his will he gave her his personal chattels, worth £900; a legacy of £250; and a life interest in one half of his residuary estate, such life interest being estimated to produce £600 a year. Subject to the life interest, he left his residuary estate to his brother and sister. He also exercised a right under a Deed of Partnership with his brother, which provided that, in the event of the death of a partner leaving a widow or a fiancée or other person nominated by him in his will to receive an annuity, the surviving partner should pay to such person during their joint lives an annuity of £500, subject to abatement if the net profits of the business should be less than £3,000 in any year. The annuity was liable to cease altogether on the happening of certain contingencies, including the death of the surviving partner. The Court held that it was not reasonable to subject the applicant's future income to these uncertainties, and ordered that an annuity of £500 a year should be paid out of the income of the residuary estate during her widowhood, with a proviso that no part of it should be payable except to the extent that it was not received under the Partnership Deed.

Re Ducksbury [1966] 1 W.L.R. 1226

The applicant was the daughter of the testator by his first wife. She had been a beneficiary under a settlement made by him, but the only direct payment she had received from it was £677 when it was wound up in 1955. The testator had parted from his first wife in great bitterness, and with her encouragement the applicant had written a letter to him which was intended to, and did, wound him. The applicant later sought a reconciliation, but without success. He died in 1961, leaving all his £16,000 estate to his second wife. The applicant was unmarried and able to earn her living as a secretary, but preferred to work part-time and pursue part-time studies. The Court held that, although the testator's primary duty was to his second wife, he did owe some moral obligation to the applicant, and she should have £2 a week from the estate during her life, until she married.

Re Dyer The Times March 13, 1964

The applicant was the widow of the testator. They had married in 1911, and had separated for good in 1920. At the time of the separation the testator gave the applicant the lease and goodwill of a grocer's shop, which she sold because it was unprofitable. Subsequently he provided her with accommodation in a property of his, paying the rates and her fuel and electricity bills, but giving her nothing else. Her only income at the time of the application was the old age pension. By his will he in effect divided his estate between the woman with whom he had been living, his illegitimate daughter by another woman, and his daughter by the applicant. The Court awarded the applicant £7 a week out of the estate.

Re E [1966] 1 W.L.R. 709

The applicant was the widow of the testator. She had married him in 1925, and he deserted her in 1941, going to live with another woman, the Defendant, with whom he remained until his death, and by whom he had three (or possibly four) children. In 1951 he conveyed the former matrimonial home to the applicant. In 1953 he conveyed to the other woman the house in which they were living together. He left his whole estate of about £1,000 to the other woman; most of this was derived from a grant from his employers, earned while he was living with her. At the time of his death he was paying the Plaintiff £1 a week, but this ceased on his death; she also had a state pension, and a small income from letting lodgings in the former matrimonial home, which latter items of income continued after his death. The Court, influenced by the smallness of the estate and the testator's moral obligation to the Defendant, dismissed the application, but with no order for costs save a legal aid taxation.

Re Elliott The Times May 18, 1956

The applicant was the widow of the testator, who made no provision for her out of his estate of £2,670. She was aged 48, an epileptic, and had capital of £967, the widow's pension of £2 a week, and earnings of £1 a week as a shop assistant. It was argued that she ought to receive nothing, because the widow's pension made her better off than she had been in the lifetime of the testator. However, the Court awarded her such a lump sum as would produce an annuity of 15s. a week. (The entitlement under the will does not appear from the report.)

Re Eyre [1968] 1 W.L.R. 530

The applicant was the former wife of the testator, and was 63 years old. She married him in 1925, had two children by him, and divorced him in 1946, on the ground of his adultery with the woman whom he subsequently married, and who was left his widow when he died in 1964. At his death he was paying the applicant £1,500 a year secured maintenance, and a further £2,000 a year for their joint lives, both less tax. The gross estate was worth about £500,000, but was subject to heavy estate duty. Its major asset had increased greatly in value since the divorce. The chief beneficiaries under the will were the testator's widow, and his two children by the applicant. The children were financially well established, and were content that any periodical payments ordered to be made to the applicant should reduce their entitlement, and not affect that of the widow. The Court held that an order for secured maintenance ought not to be treated as a predetermination of what a survivor should receive after the death of a former spouse; that there could not be any general rule that a first wife should be accorded financial equality with a widow; that, contrariwise, a lack of parity between the financial position of a first and a second wife during the lifetime of the husband should not of itself be treated as a sufficient reason for prolonging that position after his death; and that, assuming that the former wife's needs and her means remained as they were before the husband's death, and assuming that the net estate was sufficient for the purpose, then it was reasonable that she should continue to receive the same provision as during the husband's lifetime, sufficiency being determined having regard to the provision for or needs of other claimants on the husband's bounty. Applying these principles to the facts of the case, the Court concluded that it would have been reasonable for the deceased to have made provision for the applicant's maintenance; that the provision in fact made was not reasonable; and that, while it would not be appropriate to put the applicant on an equal footing with the widow, a reasonable provision for her would be the amount she was receiving prior to the death of the deceased.

(This case should now be read in the light of *Re Crawford*, noted above under the Inheritance (Provision for Family and Dependants) Act, 1975.)

Re F (1965) 109 S.J. 212

The applicant was the former wife of the testator. They had married in 1928 and divorced in 1947. By his will he left his estate of £6,000 to his widow, whom he married in 1948. She also received benefits of about £21,000 under insurance policies taken out by him, and an *ex gratia* payment of £3,300 a year, less tax, for five years, from the Company of which he had been managing director. The applicant had been receiving £1,100 a year maintenance, less tax. This ceased when the testator died. She was 59, in poor health, and had an income of about £8 a week. The Court awarded her £650 a year out of the estate, which was in excess of its income; the Court was prepared to have it exhausted in this way.

Re Ferrar's Application [1966] P. 126

In this case the Court of Appeal held that there was no power to make an interim order in favour of a former spouse in proceedings under this jurisdiction. The power to do so was subsequently given to the Court by the Family Provision Act 1966.

Re Franks [1948] Ch. 62

The applicant, Peter Franks, was a child of the testatrix by her second husband. By her will made in 1940 she had given her second husband a legacy of £1,000 and the residue of her estate to Richard Brandt, her child by her first husband, on his attaining 21. She died two days ofter giving birth to Peter. Richard had left school, and hoped to go on to University. The Court considered that reasonable financial provision had not been made for Peter, and that the Summons should be adjourned until Richard attained full age. At that time Richard might agree to an arrangement which would dispose of the whole matter. Failing that, the Court could either deal with the matter finally then, or adjourn the Summons for a longer period.

Re Gale [1966] Ch. 236

On an application to vary an existing order, the Court of Appeal held that periodic payments under the Inheritance (Family Provision) Act 1938 had to be uniform payments of a specified amount, and not payments of a variable fraction of the whole of the annual income of the estate. This is no longer so: section 3, Family Provision Act 1966; section 2, Inheritance (Provision for Family and Dependants) Act 1975. The Court of Appeal also made observations on changes in circumstances between the original order and the application for a variation of it, and these observations may still have relevance; for example, Russell L.J. observed that a dependant will not ordinarily be penalised for thrift.

Re Goard (1962) 106 S.J. 721

The applicant was the widow of the testator. They had married in 1948, and separated in 1952, when the applicant's claim for maintenance was dismissed by the justices. However, from then until his death the testator paid her £1 a week for their illegitimate daughter. He left his net estate of about £2,500 to his parents or the survivor of them, "in the sure knowledge that [they] will make adequate provision for my daughter." When the testator died the applicant and the daughter were on national assistance. The Court held that, had the daughter not been in the picture, the applicant's claim would have been dismissed. However, because of her the applicant would be awarded £500, with interest from the date of the order, to be her own money and not held in trust for the daughter.

[The daughter could not apply under the law as it then stood, because she was illegitimate.]

Re Goodwin [1969] 1 Ch. 283

The applicant was the widow of the testator. They had enjoyed 25 years of happy marriage. He made his will after discussing its terms with her. He gave her a legacy of £100, his personal chattels, and the residue. Both of them believed that the residue would be worth between £8,000 and £9,000. It turned out to be worth about £1,860. The Court held that the reasonableness of the dispositions of an estate had to be judged objectively, not subjectively, and awarded the Plaintiff periodical payments of £8 a week, determinable on remarriage (the express terms of the Inheritance (Provision for Family and Dependants) Act 1975, render much of the judgment obsolete).

Re Greaves [1954] 1 W.L.R. 760

This case was concerned with the restrictions on the Court's discretion to extend the six-month period for application, which have now been relaxed, and with other procedural points. The applicant was the widow of the testator.

Re Greenham The Times, December 2, 1964

The applicant was the widow of the deceased. They had been separated since 1954. Under the separation agreement he had paid her £65 a month, and he had also given her a house. Since his death she had received £952 a year from an insurance taken out in 1928 with money provided by him. His estate had a gross value of £400,000 or so, and £263,000 duty had been paid on it. He gave most of it to charity. The Court awarded the applicant an annuity of £1,000 a year gross.

Re Gregory [1970] 1 W.L.R. 1455

The applicant was the widow of the testator. She had married him in 1916, but he deserted her in about 1926, and they never lived together thereafter, although he asked her to do so. Apart from £100 which he gave her on one occasion towards her fare to the United States to visit their daughter, she never received any money from him after his desertion. He left his net estate of about £2,800 to 17 members of his family and friends. The County Court Judge dismissed the application, and the Court of Appeal dismissed an appeal, but making no order as to the widow's costs. The Court of

Appeal was especially influenced by the small size of the estate, and the fact that the applicant had not been dependent upon the deceased.

Re H. [1975] Fam. Law 172

The applicant was the minor child of the deceased, who had married the child's mother in 1965. That marriage had been annulled in 1969. The deceased died intestate in 1973. His only asset was a half share in the leasehold of the flat which was his matrimonial home with his second wife. The half share was valued at £3,500. The Court made a lump sum order of £2,000, charged on the half share, with enforcement deferred until further notice.

Re Harker-Thomas [1969] P. 28

The applicant was the former wife of the deceased. They had married in 1919, separated in or about 1928, and were divorced in 1935. The net estate was worth £6,082. It passed as on the deceased's intestacy (the second wife, the beneficiary under his will, having predeceased him) to relatives with whom he had enjoyed no recent contact, but who were all far more needy than the applicant, who was "comfortably off." She was receiving £3.10s.0d a week from the deceased at the time of his death. The Court held that, while the claims of the relatives on the deceased were weakened by the absence of recent contact and of close or contemporary affection, the ties of blood and the rights provided by the law of intestacy ought not to be disregarded; and that it was not unreasonable, upon consideration of all the factors including the possibility that the *inter vivos* maintenance might have been stopped had the deceased known of the applicant's better financial position, for no provision to have been made for the applicant by the will. Therefore her application was dismissed. The costs order is not reported.

Re Hills [1941] W.N. 123

The applicant was the widow of the testator. He had not lived with her for several years. He left his estate, which had a gross value of £4,724.0s.11d., between another lady and his children. The Court ordered that two-thirds of the actual income produced by the residuary estate (exclusive of property specifically bequeathed) be paid to the applicant during widowhood, but that this was not to give her any power to require realisation of any part of the estate (whether reversionary or otherwise) by the trustee or affect the provisions of the will as regarded the trustee's powers and duties to realise or postpone the realisation of any part of the property. The order was made subject to the condition that the applicant should inform the trustee of any income to which she might become legally entitled and of any property to which she might become legally entitled in possession except property not exceeding £100 vesting at the same time and from a single source and except accumulations of income belonging to the applicant and except property purchased for value by her out of her own moneys and except movables, chattels and effects of household, domestic or personal use or ornament.

Re Hodgkinson [1967] Ch. 634

This case in the Court of Appeal was concerned with the restrictions on the Court's discretion to extend the six-month period for application, which have now been relaxed. The applicant was the widow of the testator.

Re Hodgkinson The Times, October 25, 1956

This case was likewise concerned with the restrictions on the Court's discretion to extend the time for application, which have now been relaxed. The applicant was the widow of the testator.

Re Howell [1953] 1 W.L.R. 1034

The applicants were the minor children of the testator. When he made his will they were living with him and his second wife; he and their mother, his first wife, had been divorced. After his death they returned to their mother. The testator left all his estate to his second wife; it was worth about £2,500, and included the matrimonial home. The application was dismissed. (The Court of Appeal appears to have applied the subjective test of reasonableness, and the case might well not be followed today. The Court was influenced by the fact that the testator could be said to have acted reasonably in leaving his estate to his second wife when his children by his first wife were living with his second wife.)

Re Inns [1947] Ch. 576

The applicant was the widow of the testator. He left an estate of £607,780. His will permitted the applicant to reside in the matrimonial home so long as she should remain his widow, and gave her the income of £85,000 during her widowhood. She contended that the will did not make reasonable financial provision for her, because her income was insufficient for her to continue to live at the matrimonial home, as the testator intended. The Court dismissed the application, but ordered that the costs of all parties taxed as between solicitor and client should be paid out of the estate. The judgment contains observations about the nature of the family provision jurisdiction which are still of relevance.

Re Jackson [1952] 2 T.L.R. 90

The applicant was the widow of the testator. They had married in 1910, and separated in 1919. He left a net estate of more than £93,000, of which £59,000 was given in legacies to charities; £6,000 remained in residue, and he gave that to charity as well. He gave the applicant a life annuity of £150 clear of death duties. The Court awarded her an additional annuity of £450 a year during widowhood, and directed that the fund to provide for it should come ratably from the legacies to the charities and the residue, that is to say as to 59/65ths from the former and 6/65ths from the latter.

Re Jennery [1967] Ch. 280

The applicant was the widow of the testator. By his will he gave all his estate, worth nearly £1,100, to his two daughters, who took out letters of administration with the will annexed. The trial judge awarded her a lump sum of £600. The two daughters failed to give effect to the order, and the widow sought to enforce it as if it were an order for the payment of money. The Court of Appeal held that the order could not be enforced in that way. It merely made the successful applicant the equivalent of a beneficiary under a will, who could take the measures for enforcement open to a beneficiary.

Re John (1967) 111 S.J. 15

This case was concerned with the restrictions on the Court's discretion to extend the six-month period for application, which have now been relaxed. The applicant was the widow of the testator. At the testator's funeral his son had made certain representations to her about the provision she could have, and in reliance upon that she had not applied to the Court in time. The Court attributed some significance to this.

Re Joslin [1941] Ch. 200

The applicant was the widow of the testator, who left his estate of about £370 to the woman with whom he had been living and her children by him. By the death of the testator the applicant lost the £1 a week which he had been paying her, but she retained a small income from property and from taking boarders. The beneficiaries were penniless. The Court held that the testator owed duties to both the applicant and the beneficiaries, and in the light of the small size of the estate, and the financial circumstances of the applicant and the beneficiaries, was entitled to act as he had done. Accordingly the application was dismissed with costs.

Re Kay [1965] 1 W.L.R. 1463

This case was concerned with the restrictions on the Court's discretion to extend the six-month period for application, which have now been relaxed. The applicant was the widow of the testator.

Re Knowles [1966] Ch. 386

In this case the Court held that it had no jurisdiction to sanction a compromise under the Inheritance (Family Provision) Act 1938 on behalf of persons of full age and capacity who were not parties to the proceedings. The Court now has such power in applications under the Inheritance (Provision for Family and Dependants) Act, 1975, because Order 99, rule 4(2) of the Rules of the Supreme Court applies Order 15, rule 13 to such proceedings.

Lamerton v. The Personal Representatives of Lamerton (1966) 110 S.J. 288

The applicant was the former wife of the deceased. They had married in 1918, and the marriage had been annulled in 1935. The Court held that it had jurisdiction, and ordered the respondents to pay the applicant £750 a year, less tax. The report does not state the value of the estate, nor the identity or circumstances of the beneficiaries.

Re Langley The Times, June 26, 1964

The applicant was the widow of the testator. They had married in or about 1946, when the testator was about 68. He had been married before. He died in 1961, leaving his net estate of a little over £3,000 as to £800 to the applicant, and as to the rest to pecuniary legatees. She was living on national assistance. The Court expressed the view that when a husband married late in life and had a small estate and also had children it could not be his duty to leave everything to his wife. However, the Court awarded the applicant an additional lump sum of £700.

Re Lavender (1964) 108 S.J. 879

The applicant was the widow of the testator. They had married late in life, and had stayed together for less than 2 years. During that time the testator transferred a substantial part of the capital into their joint names. After the separation she obtained a maintenance order against him, and by proceedings under the Married Womens Property Act 1882 their joint capital was divided, and she received £2,610. The testator left all his net estate of about £3,440 after payment of duty to his brother and sister. The applicant was, apparently, without an income, having spent or given away all the £2,610, apart from some of it which she had used to buy a house. The major asset of the estate was the testator's own house, in which his brother was living. The Court awarded the applicant £1.1s.0d. a week.

Re Lawes (1946) 62 T.L.R. 231

The applicant was the widower of the testatrix. Her estate was worth £4,500, but she gave the applicant no more than £200, and furniture worth £50. The residue went to the R.S.P.C.A. Nothing could, apparently, be said against the widower as a husband; he was over 70, and had only a small income. The Court directed that he should receive £1 a week out of the estate until his death or remarriage.

Re Lecoche (1967) 111 S.J. 136

The applicant was the widow of the testator. They had married in 1947, and had had three sons, two of whom were still in school at the date of the application. In 1958 the testator deserted the applicant, and went to live with another woman, who bore him an illegitimate son. Under a maintenance order he was paying the applicant £4 a week, and £2 for each child. He left all his estate to his illegitimate son; after testamentary expenses and the costs of the proceedings its estimated value was about £5,000. It consisted almost entirely of a reversionary interest, and the house in which the illegitimate son and his mother were living. On the testator's death the trustees of his employers pension fund divided £6,000 equally between the applicant and the mother of the illegitimate child. The Court said that the case was one of a man supporting two families during his life, whose estate was not large enough to continue supporting them after his death. He had provided for the applicant indirectly, through the pension fund and the state widows pension. Therefore no provision would be ordered for her. Provision of £1.10s.0d. a week was ordered for each of her two sons at school, to last until they were 16.

Re Lidington [1940] Ch. 927

The applicant was the widow of the testator. They had separated in or before 1937, and he was paying her £130 a year free of tax under a separation deed. The Court held that the obligation thereunder ended on his death. He gave her nothing by his will. The eventual value of his estate was uncertain. The Court ordered that the applicant should have two thirds of the income of the estate (the statutory limit at that time), upon her undertaking to maintain her children by the testator thereout. She and the trustee of the estate were given liberty to apply.

Re Lofts [1968] 1 W.L.R. 1949

The applicant was the widow of the testator. A compromise was proposed, and the Court suggested a way in which it could be carried into effect despite the absence of certain beneficiaries. The suggestion is probably of little relevance now that Order 99, rule 4(2) of the Rules of the Supreme Court applies Order 15 rule 13.

Lusternik v. Lusternik [1972] Fam. 125

The applicant was the former wife of the deceased. They were married in 1947 and divorced in 1951. After the divorce she was awarded £6 a week maintenance, less tax. He died in 1964. By his will he gave a legacy of £500 to the applicant, another legacy of £500 elsewhere, and the residue of his estate to his daughter by his first marriage. The net estate was worth £11,608. The daughter was self-supporting, but the applicant was unable to work by reason of ill-health. The trial judge awarded her £6 a week, which the Court of Appeal increased to £8 a week. The Court of Appeal incidentally observed that the extent to which an order should be backdated in family provison proceedings was a matter of discretion in each case, although the Courts ought to guard against backdating an order for periodical payments to such extent as in effect to award an unintended lump sum.

Re M [1968] P. 174

The applicant was the former wife of the deceased. During his life there was an agreement between them whereby he paid her a lump sum, she undertook to make no further claim for maintenance against him or his estate, an existing order for maintenance was discharged, and an application by her to vary it was dismissed. After his death she applied for provision out of his estate, and the court held that it had jurisdiction to consider whether to make an order, despite the agreement and the order which had given effect to it.

Re Maclaglen The Times, March 12, 1953

The applicant was the widow of the testator. They had married in

1923, and separated in 1929. However, she had assisted him financially in subsequent years. He left his net estate of about £3,500 to the woman defendant with whom he had lived for some 8 years before death, and who had also given him money. The Court, with regret, considered that it could make no order for provision in favour of the applicant, because of the relative financial resources of the parties and the smallness of the estate. However, it ordered that the applicant's costs, taxed on the solicitor and client basis, be paid out of the estate.

Re McNare [1964] 1 W.L.R. 1255

This case was concerned with the restrictions of the Court's discretion to extend the six-month period for application, which have now been relaxed. The applicant was the widow of the testator.

Re Makein [1955] Ch. 194

In this case the Court held that an illegitimate son of a deceased person was not qualified to claim under the Inheritance (Family Provision) Act, 1938. The law is otherwise under the Inheritance (Provision for Family and Dependants) Act, 1975, by virtue of the Family Law Reform Act 1969.

Re Mason (1975) 5 Fam. Law 124

The applicant was the widow of the testator. They had married in August 1971, when they were both 61. By his will the testator gave his net estate, worth about £10,500 (including the matrimonial home valued at £6,000) to his four children, but directed his trustee to allow the applicant to live in the matrimonial home. She could not afford to do so. The Court held that the testator had not made reasonable financial provision for her, and ordered that she be given a life interest in the matrimonial home, so as to make her tenant for life thereof under the Settled Land Act 1925. Should she sell the matrimonial home, its proceeds of sale were ordered to be applied in the purchase of another house for her, and she was to have the income of any balance. The Court also ordered that she have the income of £1,500, but that any income from the proceeds of sale of the matrimonial home be set off against the income of that £1,500.

Mastaka v. Midland Bank Executor and Trustee Company Ltd. [1941] Ch. 192

The applicant was the adult unmarried daughter of the testatrix, who left a gross estate of £1,489.18s.0d. From the applicant's babyhood she had been in the care of a woman other than the testatrix, and from the age of five had never received or sought financial assistance from the testatrix. Her earning ability was limited by reason of her state of health. The application was dismissed with costs, on the ground that the applicant had not established that the testatrix had died domiciled in England; and also on the ground that the testatrix was under no obligation to the applicant on the facts.

Re Miller [1969] 1 W.L.R. 583

This was an application by the widow of the deceased, made more than four years after a grant of probate in common form, but less than six months after the grant had been affirmed in solemn form. The Court held that the six-month period for application ran from the grant in common form, and that the time would not be extended (the relevant provision allowing the Court to extend the time is now different, but the Court's remark that an Originating Summons could have been issued, and then adjourned, probably still has some relevance).

Millward v. Shenton [1972] 1 W.L.R. 711

The applicant was the adult son of the testratrix. He was unable to earn his own living by reason of illness, and was dependent on state benefits. The testatrix left her net estate of £3,144 to charity. The County Court judge dismissed the application, but the Court of Appeal awarded the applicant 11/12ths of the estate, ordering his costs and those of the executor on appeal to be paid by the charity, and the costs below on a party and party basis to come out of the estate.

Re Minter [1967] 3 All E.R. 412

The applicant was the former wife of the deceased. On an application to vary her maintenance during his life, a consent order was made under which she undertook to make no further claim for maintenance against him or his estate. The Court held that this did not prevent her applying after his death. The law is probably the same under the Inheritance (Provision for Family and Dependants) Act 1975, although under section 15 thereof the Court has in divorce proceedings a power to bar applications under the Act.

Re Morris The Times, April 14, 1967

The applicant was the widow of the testator. They married in 1947, and had ceased to live together some six months later. The husband began proceedings for annulment, but discontinued them. By his will he only gave the Plaintiff £250, but she became entitled to a pension of £900 a year from his employers. The estate was worth about £26,000 net. The Court held that the failure of the applicant to be a good loving wife had to be taken into account, and that, although the husband had acted with great generosity to her and her son throughout the marriage, that was no measure of reasonable provision after his death. The application was dismissed. The costs order is not reported.

Re Nesbitt The Times, November 22, 1963

The applicant was the widow of the testator, who left his whole estate, except £50, to his son. The estate after the payment of testamentary expenses and the executor's costs of the family provision application was worth no more than £1,600, and consisted mainly of the matrimonial home, in which the son was living. The Court said it would have liked to have given the widow £3 a week charged on the house, and allow the son to continue to live there, but could not do so (because of the terms of the 1938 Act before its subsequent amendment). The Court awarded the applicant the whole of the estate as a lump sum payment.

Re Parkinson The Times, October 3, 1975

The applicant was the widow of the testator. They had married in 1961, when he was 65 and she 49. His estate consisted of the matrimonial home, valued at £3,500; furniture and effects worth £100; and £300 in cash. By his will he gave the applicant a life interest in the house and effects so long as she did not marry and lived in it alone, with a gift over to the R.S.P.C.A. The trial judge dismissed the application. The costs of the hearing before him were such that the house had to be sold. Because of this, the Court of Appeal allowed the widow's appeal by giving her the net proceeds of sale of the house as a lump sum. The Court expressed concern over the effect, apparently unavoidable though it was, of the burden of costs on such a small estate.

Re Parry The Times, April 19, 1956

The applicant was the widower of the testatrix, who left her estate of £2,684 among her own relatives. He was aged 84, and lived in an old people's home. The Court ordered that he should have 10s. a week out of the estate.

Re Peete [1952] W.N. 306

The Plaintiff claimed to be the widow of the testator, her alleged second husband. The Court held that the burden of proof was on her to show that she was his widow. She relied upon her marriage certificate, in which she was described as a widow. However, she was unable to produce the death certificate of her first husband, or otherwise adduce satisfactory evidence of his death. Nor on the evidence could she rely on the presumption of death after disappearance over a long period. Therefore the Court dismissed her application.

Re Pointer [1946] Ch. 324

The applicant was the unmarried daughter of the testatrix, and the Court ordered that she be paid 30s. a week. A point arose on the bearing of certain tax legislation on this. The Court held that a person in whose favour an order was made under the Inheritance (Family Provision) Act 1938 was placed for all purposes in the position of the beneficiary, and that the effect of the order was to vary the will in question (see also as to this *Re Jennery*, above).

Re Pringle The Times, February 2, 1956

The Plaintiff was the adult son of the testatrix, who left her net estate of some £2,291 to two friends. He was a mentally defective patient in hospital. The Court awarded him 10s. a week out of the estate, for "comforts."

Re Pugh [1943] Ch. 387

The applicant was the widow of the testator. He left a farm worth about £5,000 to his grandson, and his residue worth about £1,800 to the applicant, who was his sole executrix. The Court took into account the fact that the applicant and the testator had been married for a short time only; and that she appeared to have made no contribution to the prosperity of the farm, while the grandson's father had. Therefore, although the Court would itself have made somewhat greater provision for her had it been the testator, it dismissed her application, making no order for costs.

Re Ralphs [1968] 1 W.L.R. 1522

This was an application by a widow, which was compromised at the hearing. During the hearing it emerged that the applicant and one of the defendants had suffered hardship because no payments had been made to them, and the Court gave guidance to avoid that situation in the future (as to the terms of this guidance, see the text of this book at p. 12). The observations of Vaisey J. in *Re Simson*, below, were to some extent disapproved.

Re Riglar The Times, October 18, 1956

The applicant was the widow of the testator. They had married in 1947, when he was 74 and she was 70. He left all his estate, worth £5,323 gross, to charities. She had an income of £1.7s.9d. a week, owned a bungalow valued at £750, and had a small sum in the Post Office Savings Bank. The Court directed that the whole income of the residuary estate be paid to her during widowhood.

Roberts v. Roberts [1964] 1 W.L.R. 560

The applicant was the former wife of the testator, who had married him in 1928 and divorced him in 1954. He left all his estate to his second wife. It consisted of a half share in a greengrocery business; the share in the goodwill was estimated at £1,000, and the share in the freehold premises on which the business was carried on was estimated at £5,000. The applicant had only the state pension and national assistance. The widow had the same, and also £1 a week from her first husband, who lodged with her. The Court awarded the applicant 15s. a week, which could be increased on the sale of the freehold and might be an incentive to the co-owner of the business to find a purchaser for it.

Re Rodwell [1970] Ch. 726

This case decided that a married daughter whose marriage had been annulled was qualified to claim under the Inheritance (Family Provision) Act, 1938. It would appear to have no relevance under the Inheritance (Provision for Family and Dependants) Act 1975, which gives daughters a right to claim whatever their age and whether or not they have married.

Re Ruttie [1970] 1 W.L.R. 89

A widow applicant sought to have the six-month time limit for applications extended. The Court held that it would be premature to lay down principles to guide the decision whether or not to extend the time (the power to do so had only become unfettered in 1966). Instead, the Court regarded all the circumstances of the case, to see whether it was reasonably clear that an extension of time was required in the interests of justice (see now *Re Salmon*; *Re Adams*; and *Escritt v. Escritt*; above).

Re S [1965] P. 165

The applicant was the former wife of the deceased. During his life there was a consent order whereby her claim for maintenance was dismissed (she had a business partnership with him). After his death, the Court held that this dismissal did not necessarily prevent the Court awarding her provision from his estate.

Re Sanderson The Times, November 1, 1977

The applicant was the widow of the testator. She was 80 years old. They had married in 1916, and had had two children, but the testator had left her in about 1920. He had paid her maintenance, but this was reduced over time, and ceased in 1961. When he died in 1963 the applicant discovered that he had become a man of considerable means; after the payment of estate duty and pecuniary legacies there was more than £50,000 left in the estate. By his will he gave it all to charity. The Court awarded the applicant £1,000 a year during her widowhood. She had some income of her own, but the Court observed that she might wish to live in comfort, with domestic help and private medical care.

Re Searle [1949] Ch. 73

The applicant widow applied before probate had been granted. The Court held that this did not invalidate her application. The Court also held that, if a testator had given a reason in his will for his failure to make provision for an applicant, the Court could nevertheless admit evidence to show that he had other reasons.

Re Shanahan [1973] Fam. 1, Fam. Div.

The applicant was the former wife of the deceased. She married him in 1937, and had four children by him. She divorced him in 1956, and in 1965 he remarried. At the time of his death he was paying her £400 a year maintenance. Apart from two legacies totalling £500, he left all his estate of about £14,000 to his second wife. Much of the judgment is taken up with the question whether the test of reasonable financial provision is subjective or objective, a question now decided in favour of objectivity. The Court observed that the claims of the applicant on the bounty of the deceased arose from her having borne him a large family while having undergone ill treatment at his hands; from her having, after their parting, brought up their children on exiguous resources; from her poor state of health; and from her lack of means compared with the widow. The Court confirmed the Registrar's award of a lum sum of £7,000, and her costs out of the estate. The result was that the applicant, aged 56, had capital of £7,000 (out of the estate) and an income by way of state pension of £250 a year. The widow, aged 64, had capital of £15,350 (£8,350 of her own and £7,000 from the estate) and income from other sources of £1,100 a year.

Re Simson [1950] Ch. 38

The applicant was the widow of the testator. They had married in 1910, and had entered into a deed of separation in 1929, under which she had received £200 a year until his death. His net estate was worth about £14,000. Under his will, in the events that happened, the widow received £2,600. The Court awarded her £87 a year more, during widowhood. The judge said that he would have liked to have given her £96 a year, but £9 of that he would have charged on legacies which had already been paid as a result of her expressly abandoning any claim against them at an earlier stage in the proceedings. (The case contains observations about the unwisdom of the executors making any distributions before the final hearing, but these are obsolete in the light of *Re Ralphs*, above.)

Re Sivyer [1967] 1 W.L.R. 1482

The applicant was the minor unmarried daughter, aged 15, of the deceased, by his second wife. He died intestate, and all his estate of slightly over £4,000 passed to his third wife, who had married him in 1959 and left him in 1961. The principal asset of the estate was the proceeds of sale of a dwelling-house, which had been bought, at least in part, out of the savings of the applicant's mother. The applicant was without means; the widow appeared to be unemployed, and had very little money. The Court awarded the applicant a lump sum of £2,500.

Re Smallwood [1951] Ch. 369

In this case, which was an application by a widow, the Court held that its power under the Inheritance (Family Provision) Act 1938 to consider evidence of a testator's reasons for his dispositions was not restricted to reasons actually given by him for making them.

Re Smythe The Times, December 10, 1966

The applicant had married the testator in 1937, and he left her in 1942. There was no divorce. He paid her a varying sum by way of maintenance; it was £6 a week when he died. He left his net estate of £1,260 to his mother, and the benefit of an insurance policy to the woman with whom he had been living. As a result of his death the applicant received a pension from his employer, and a widow's allowance from the Army; the pension and the allowance were more than £6 a week in total. The Court dismissed the application, stating *inter alia* that it would require a greater disparity between the receipts of the applicant before and after the testator's death to justify disturbing his will. The costs order does not appear to be reported.

Re Snowdon The Times, May 13, 1966

The applicant was the widow of the testator. They had married in 1921, and had had three children, but he had left her in 1946. He did not support her thereafter. By his will he gave his whole estate to a friend of many years standing, who had helped him considerably. The Court made a lump sum order of £1,500 (the value of the estate is not given in the report).

Re Stone (1970) 114 S.J. 36, C.A.

The applicant was the widow of the deceased. The case is only reported on her application for leave to apply out of time. The deceased had made substantial *inter vivos* gifts to her, and also made substantial provision for her by his will. However, sometime after probate had been granted it emerged that estate duty would by payable at 65 per cent. on both the estate and the gifts. Thereupon the applicant consulted independent solicitors. They arranged friendly discussions with the executor's solicitors, but did not issue an application until three weeks and one day after the six-month time limit had expired. The trial judge considered that the application was hopeless, so refused to extend the time. The Court of Appeal held that there was an arguable case, and therefore extended the time.

Re Styler [1942] Ch. 387

The applicant was the widower of the testatrix, who left an estate of about £1,200. They had agreed to make wills in one another's favour, but she had subsequently made a will giving all her estate to her daughter by her first husband. In the light of these facts, and the facts that the widower was earning an income of about the same of that of the daughter and her husband, the Court dismissed the application. The costs order is not reported.

Re Sylvester [1941] Ch. 87

The applicant was the widower of the testatrix, who left a net estate of about £19,000. By her will she gave most of it to her relatives, and to charities; she gave an annuity of £52 a year to the applicant. The Court expressed the view that applications by husbands should not readily be entertained, but the circumstances of the particular case were somewhat exceptional. On his marriage the applicant had given up his employment; he had looked after the house, and nursed the testatrix when she was ill. The Court ordered an additional £3 a week be paid to him during his widowhood.

Re Talbot [1962] 1 W.L.R. 1113

The applicant was the former wife of the testator. She had married him in 1937, and a decree of nullity had been pronounced in 1946. In 1947 maintenance was ordered for their joint lives in the sum of £432 a year gross. In 1950 the testator remarried, and subsequently had three children by his second wife. He died in 1960, leaving all his estate to his second wife. Its net value after payment of duty was £19,397. The applicant had capital of £743, and a total income of £500, partly from employment. The widow had capital of £1,293, apart from her interest under the will. The two elder children were boarding at a fee-paying school; this was desirable, by reason of their state of health. For health reasons also the widow could not take employment. The Court held that the widow's claim on the testator was paramount, and dismissed the application, making no order in respect of the applicant's costs, and ordering the costs of the childrens' guardian *ad litem* to be paid out of the estate.

Re Thornley [1969] 1 W.L.R. 1037

The applicant, aged 59, was the widow of the testator. She had married him in 1948, and had left him in 1962, for justifiable reasons. Thereafter he paid her £5 a week. In 1963 the third defendant began to live with him. He treated her badly. In 1966 he killed himself. His net estate was valued at £16,000 and its major asset was a public house and adjoining land. Under his will, in the events that had happened, the applicant received an annuity of £416 a year, and the third defendant a legacy of £1,000 and the public house and land. The trial judge awarded the applicant an initial £100 a year until her death or remarriage. The Court of Appeal increased the £100 to £234, so that the applicant would have a total income of £900 (£416 + £234 + the state widows' pension, then worth about £250 a year).

Re Trott [1958] 1 W.L.R. 604

A posthumous daughter of the testator applied under the 1938 Act, and asked for an extension of time, which was granted, under the somewhat restrictive provision for extension which was then operative.

Re Trowell The Times, November 29, 1957

The applicant was the widow of the testator. He had married her in 1915, and left her in 1924. There were no children. During the separation years he paid her maintenance, apparently of £1 a week throughout, except between 1926 and 1954, when he had made her a further allowance of £1.5s.0d. a week. Since 1925 he had lived with another woman, to whom he had (apparently) left his whole estate. Its major asset was a bungalow, which he had bought with the help of the other woman's life savings, and which she was still living. The Court made an order for payment to the applicant of 2s. a week, intended as a derisory order.

Re Vrint [1940] Ch. 920

The applicant was the widow of the testator, who left a net estate of £138.14s.10d. They had married in 1914, and had been separated by 1935 at the latest. The applicant was 58 years old, and her only income was the pension of 10s. a week. The Court dismissed the application with costs, on the ground that the Inheritance (Family Provision) Act, 1938 was passed to provide maintenance and not legacies, and that in the instant case the estate was too small to provide maintenance. On a procedural point, the Court also held that "evidence" under section 1(7) of the Act was not confined to legal evidence.

Re W (1975) 119 S.J. 439

The applicant was the former wife of the deceased. They had married in 1934, when she was 34 and he 28. In 1946 she divorced him, and did not apply for financial provision. He died in 1972, leaving his estate of some £28,000 to two woman friends. The Court found that he had been secretive about his affairs, had never let the former wife know the extent of his wealth, and had been able to amass capital because he had not had to support her. She was 75 years old, with only the state retirement pension, and dependent upon the charity of aged relatives for her home. The beneficiaries had strong moral claims on the deceased's bounty, but were not in need of money. The applicant was awarded a lump sum of £11,000.

Re Watkins [1949] 1 All E.R. 695

The applicant was the adult daughter of the testator. Her marriage had been annulled, and she was a patient in a mental hospital. The net estate was about £23,341, and the applicant was entitled under the will to a one-third share in the residue, which one third share was estimated to yield her £72 a year. The Court held that a testator was entitled to have regard to the provision available to the applicant from the National Health Service, and to make no further provision for her. Accordingly the application was dismissed. The applicant was ordered to pay the costs on a party and party basis of one of the Defendants, a specific devisee and legatee, but not of the residuary legatees.

Re Watkins [1953] 2 All E.R. 1113

The applicant applied as the widow of the testator, her second husband, whom she had married in 1948. She could produce no documentary evidence of the death of her first husband, but she had not seen or heard from or of him since 1922. The Court held that his death could be presumed to have happened before 1948. After considering the facts (which are not fully reported) the Court doubled her annuity under the will, from £2 to £4 a week. The estate was worth about £15,000.

Re Westby [1946] W.N. 141

This was an application by an infant son of the testator, who had made no provision for him, although leaving a net estate of £8,383. The case is only reported on the form of order allocating the burden of the maintenance ordered, which was that £145 a year, being $3\frac{1}{2}$ per cent. a year on half the value of the estate, should be paid to the applicant's mother, by equal monthly payments, she undertaking to apply the same for his maintenance, and credit being allowed to the executrix for moneys already paid for maintaining the applicant in excess of such monthly sums. The order further declared that there ought to be retained until the applicant attained the age of 21 years such portion of a legacy given by the will to another defendant as when invested would produce by the income thereof the yearly sum of £25; and that such income, and in case of deficiency the capital of the retained portion, ought to be applied in payment of £25 towards the said sum of £145 in each year after the first year from the testator's death.

Re Whittle, Whittle v. *Painter* Ch.D. and C.A. March 5, 1973, C.A. transcript 73/94A

The applicant was the widow of the deceased. They had married in 1926, and separated in 1941. He paid her £2 a week from 1941 and later somewhat more. He died in 1970. During the marriage his circumstances were modest, but later they prospered. He made no provision for the applicant by his will, leaving all the residue of his estate, worth at least £60,000 or thereabouts, to his son by another woman. The trial judge awarded the applicant £1,500 a year, and the Court of Appeal dismissed with costs an appeal against this.

Re Wilson (1969) 113 S.J. 794

The applicant was the widow of the testatrix. He had married her as his second wife in 1941. From that time they had together run his business (which he had possessed before the marriage), and part of the profits had gone to her. She left her estate of about £6,000 to her brother, apart from a legacy of £100. The applicant had savings of £50, and relied on his pension and upon supplementary benefit for income. The Court awarded him £4 a week from the estate until his death or remarriage.

Index